바로 읽는
배경지식 독해

Chunjae
Makes
Chunjae

▼

[바로 읽는 배경지식 독해] LEVEL 4

기획총괄	장경률
편집개발	김윤미, 김희윤, 이민선
디자인총괄	김희정
표지디자인	윤순미, 안채리
내지디자인	디자인뮤제오
제작	황성진, 조규영

발행일	2022년 5월 15일 2판 2022년 5월 15일 1쇄
발행인	(주)천재교육
주소	서울시 금천구 가산로9길 54
신고번호	제2001-000018호
고객센터	1577-0902
교재 내용문의	(02)3282-8834

중학부터 시작하는 수능 독해 첫걸음

바로 읽는 배경지식 독해

LEVEL 4

Draw Your Future Name Card 🖊

Picture Here

My Name _____

My Job _____

How to Use

영어 독해를 잘하기 위해서는 단순히 영어 문장만 읽을 줄 안다고 해서 다 되는 것이 아닙니다.
영어 문장을 읽어도 도무지 무슨 말인지 모르는 경우가 많기 때문입니다.

바로 읽는 배경지식 독해 시리즈는 여러분의 독해 실력 향상을 위해 다음과 같이 구성하였습니다.

| 배경지식
(Background Knowledge) | + | 어휘
(Vocabulary) |

이 책을 통해 배경지식과 어휘 실력을 키워 나간다면,
수능 영어에서 출제되는 다양한 주제의 글들도 쉽게 이해할 수 있습니다.

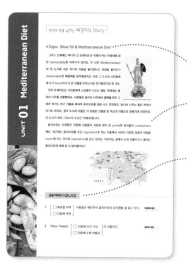

생각의 폭을 넓히는 배경지식 Story

● 재미있는 이야기를 통해, 주제에 관해 미리 생각해 보고 독해를 준비합니다.

● 읽을수록 어휘 실력도 향상됩니다. 잘 모르는 어휘는 Vocabulary에서
확인합니다.

● 본문 미리보기 **QUIZ** 를 통해 배울 내용을 간단한 퀴즈로 미리 만나보세요.

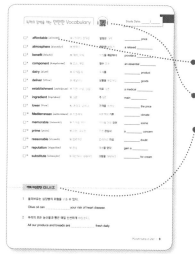

독해의 장벽을 깨는 만만한 Vocabulary

● 본문에 나오는 15개의 어휘를 미리 학습합니다.

● QR코드 제공: native speaker의 음성으로 단어를 들어보세요.

● 어휘 자신만만 **QUIZ** 를 통해 실력을 간단히 체크합니다.

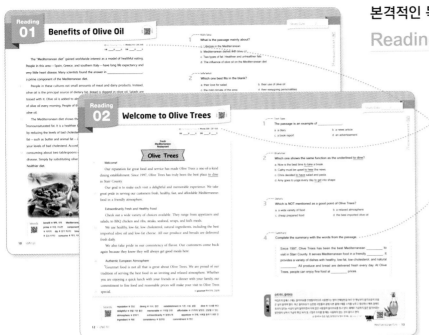

본격적인 독해 실력 향상을 위한
Reading 01, 02

- 1개의 Unit이 통합교과적 연관성을 지닌 두 개의 재미있는 이야기로 구성되어 있습니다.

- 체계적인 독해를 위한 main idea → details → summary 등과 같은 문제로 구성되어 있습니다.

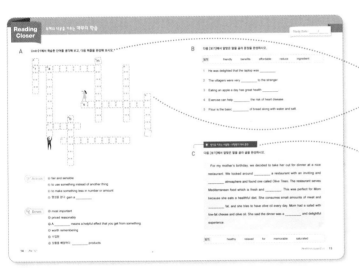

독해의 내공을 키우는 마무리 학습

- Unit에서 배운 어휘를 종합 점검합니다.

- crossword puzzle을 통한 재미있는 어휘 학습을 합니다.

🔆 생각을 키우는 서술형 · 수행평가 대비 훈련

앞에서 배운 2개의 Reading을 종합적으로 이해 및 평가합니다. 서술형 쓰기 연습을 통해 다양한 종류의 시험을 대비합니다.

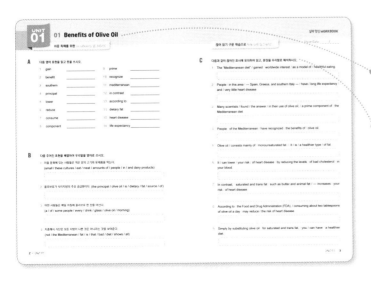

실력 향상 WORKBOOK

- 각 Reading마다 실력 향상을 위한 워크북이 제공됩니다.

- 쉬운 독해를 위한 Vocabulary와 끊어 읽기 구문 학습으로 여러분의 독해 실력을 한층 더 업그레이드 할 수 있습니다.

Table of Contents

"No person has the right to rain on your dreams."

어느 누구도 네 꿈을 훼방 놓을 권리는 없어.

마틴 루서 킹 주니어 *Martin Luther King Jr.*

Background Knowledge Reading

Self Study Management Table 자기 주도 학습 관리표

Unit	Start 공부 시작		Finish 공부 끝		Self Check				My Comment
					배경지식을 많이 쌓았어요!	어휘 실력이 늘었어요!	독해에 자신감이 +1 늘었어요!	모든 문제들을 다 풀었어요!	내 자신에게 한 마디!
01	월	일	월	일	☺ ☺ ☺	☺ ☺ ☺	☺ ☺ ☺	☺ ☺ ☺	
02	월	일	월	일	☺ ☺ ☺	☺ ☺ ☺	☺ ☺ ☺	☺ ☺ ☺	
03	월	일	월	일	☺ ☺ ☺	☺ ☺ ☺	☺ ☺ ☺	☺ ☺ ☺	
04	월	일	월	일	☺ ☺ ☺	☺ ☺ ☺	☺ ☺ ☺	☺ ☺ ☺	
05	월	일	월	일	☺ ☺ ☺	☺ ☺ ☺	☺ ☺ ☺	☺ ☺ ☺	
06	월	일	월	일	☺ ☺ ☺	☺ ☺ ☺	☺ ☺ ☺	☺ ☺ ☺	
07	월	일	월	일	☺ ☺ ☺	☺ ☺ ☺	☺ ☺ ☺	☺ ☺ ☺	
08	월	일	월	일	☺ ☺ ☺	☺ ☺ ☺	☺ ☺ ☺	☺ ☺ ☺	
09	월	일	월	일	☺ ☺ ☺	☺ ☺ ☺	☺ ☺ ☺	☺ ☺ ☺	
10	월	일	월	일	☺ ☺ ☺	☺ ☺ ☺	☺ ☺ ☺	☺ ☺ ☺	
11	월	일	월	일	☺ ☺ ☺	☺ ☺ ☺	☺ ☺ ☺	☺ ☺ ☺	
12	월	일	월	일	☺ ☺ ☺	☺ ☺ ☺	☺ ☺ ☺	☺ ☺ ☺	
13	월	일	월	일	☺ ☺ ☺	☺ ☺ ☺	☺ ☺ ☺	☺ ☺ ☺	
14	월	일	월	일	☺ ☺ ☺	☺ ☺ ☺	☺ ☺ ☺	☺ ☺ ☺	
15	월	일	월	일	☺ ☺ ☺	☺ ☺ ☺	☺ ☺ ☺	☺ ☺ ☺	
16	월	일	월	일	☺ ☺ ☺	☺ ☺ ☺	☺ ☺ ☺	☺ ☺ ☺	

My Comments에는 공부하고 나서 느낀 소감을 간단히 적어보세요.

중학부터 시작하는 수능 독해 첫걸음

바로 읽는 배경지식 독해

LEVEL 4

생각의 폭을 넓히는 **배경지식 Story**

#Topic Olive Oil & Mediterranean Diet

그리스 신화에는 바다의 신 포세이돈과 지혜의 여신 아테네에 대한 memorable한 이야기가 있어요. 두 신은 Mediterranean의 한 도시에 서로 자기의 이름을 붙이겠다고 경합을 벌이다가 reasonable한 해결책을 생각해냈어요. 바로 그 도시의 시민들에게 누가 benefit이 더 큰 선물을 주었는지로 판가름하기로 한 거죠.

먼저 포세이돈은 시민들에게 소금물이 나오는 샘을, 아테네는 올리브 나무를 선물했어요. 사람들은 올리브 나무에서 열매를 얻어 그대로 먹기도 하고 기름을 짜내어 올리브유를 얻을 수도 있었어요. 올리브 나무는 좋은 목재가 되기도 하지요. 결국 도시의 이름은 더 유용한 선물을 한 여신의 이름으로 정해지게 되었어요. 이 도시가 바로 그리스의 수도인 '아테네'랍니다.

올리브유는 오랫동안 지중해 사람들의 사랑을 받아 온 prime한 음식들의 component예요. 최근에는 올리브유를 주요 ingredient로 하는 지중해식 식단이 다양한 질병의 위험을 lower해 주는 것으로 reputation을 얻고 있어요. 이어지는 글에서 신의 선물이라고 불리는 올리브유에 대해 좀 더 알아볼까요?

본문 미리보기 **QUIZ**

1 [☐ 북유럽 지역 / ☐ 지중해 주변] 사람들은 예전부터 올리브유의 유익함을 잘 알고 있다. 10쪽에서 확인

2 Olive Trees는 [☐ 지중해 요리 식당 / ☐ 지중해 수목 박물관]의 이름이다. 12쪽에서 확인

☐ 1	**affordable** [əfɔ́ːrdəbl]	형 (가격이) 알맞은	알맞은 가격	_____ price
☐ 2	**atmosphere** [ǽtməsfiər]	명 분위기	편안한 분위기	a relaxed _____
☐ 3	**benefit** [bénəfit]	명 혜택, 이득	이점을 제공하다	provide a _____
☐ 4	**component** [kəmpóunənt]	명 요소, 부품	필수 요소	an essential _____
☐ 5	**dairy** [dɛ́ːəri]	형 유제품의	유제품	_____ products
☐ 6	**deliver** [dilívər]	동 배달하다	상품을 배달하다	_____ goods
☐ 7	**establishment** [istǽbliʃmənt]	명 기관, 시설, 설립	의료 기관	a medical _____
☐ 8	**ingredient** [ingríːdiənt]	명 성분	주성분	the main _____
☐ 9	**lower** [lóuər]	동 내리다, 낮추다	가격을 내리다	_____ the price
☐ 10	**Mediterranean** [mèdətəréiniən]	형 지중해의	지중해성 기후	a _____ climate
☐ 11	**memorable** [mémərəbl]	형 기억할 만한	기억할 만한 장면들	_____ scenes
☐ 12	**prime** [praim]	형 주된, 주요한	주된 관심사	a _____ concern
☐ 13	**reasonable** [ríːzənəbl]	형 합리적인	합리적인 의심	a _____ doubt
☐ 14	**reputation** [rèpjutéiʃən]	명 명성	명성을 얻다	gain a _____
☐ 15	**substitute** [sʌ́bstətjùːt]	동 대신하다, 대체하다	크림을 대체하다	_____ for cream

어휘 자신만만 QUIZ

1 올리브유는 심장병의 위험을 낮출 수 있다.

Olive oil can _____ your risk of heart disease.

2 우리의 모든 농산물과 빵은 매일 신선하게 배달된다.

All our produce and breads are _____ fresh daily.

Reading 01

Benefits of Olive Oil

The "Mediterranean diet" gained worldwide interest as a model of healthful eating. People in this area—Spain, Greece, and southern Italy—have long life expectancy and very little heart disease. Many scientists found the answer in _____, a prime component of the Mediterranean diet.

5 People in these cultures eat small amounts of meat and dairy products. Instead, olive oil is the principal source of dietary fat. Bread is dipped in olive oil. Salads are tossed with it. Olive oil is added to almost every dish. Some people even drink a glass of olive oil every morning. People of the Mediterranean have recognized the benefits of olive oil.

10 The Mediterranean diet shows that not all fat is bad. Olive oil consists mainly of *monounsaturated fat. It is a healthier type of fat. It can lower your risk of heart disease by reducing the levels of bad cholesterol in your blood. In contrast, *saturated and trans fat—such as butter and animal fat—increases your risk of heart disease. They increase your levels of bad cholesterol. According to the Food and Drug Administration (FDA), 15 consuming about two tablespoons of olive oil a day may reduce the risk of heart disease. Simply by substituting olive oil for saturated and trans fat, you can have a healthier diet.

* **monounsaturated fat** 단일불포화지방
* **saturated and trans fat** 포화지방과 트랜스지방

Words

benefit 명 혜택, 이득　Mediterranean 형 지중해의　gain 동 얻다　life expectancy 기대 수명, 평균 수명　prime 형 주된, 주요한　component 명 요소, 부품　dairy 형 유제품의　principal 형 주요한　dietary 형 식이의　dip 동 담가 적시다　toss 동 뒤적이다, 섞다　lower 동 낮추다, 내리다　risk 명 위험　reduce 동 감소시키다　consume 동 먹다, 마시다　substitute 동 대체하다

Main Idea

1 What is the passage mainly about?

a. Lifestyle in the Mediterranean

b. Mediterranean dishes with olive oil

c. Two types of fat: Healthier and unhealthier fats

d. The influence of olive oil on the Mediterranean diet

Inference

2 Which one best fits in the blank?

a. their love for salad

b. their use of olive oil

c. the mild climate of the area

d. their easygoing personalities

Details

3 Write T if the statement is true and F if it is false.

(1) _____ People in the Mediterranean are more likely to have heart disease than people in other areas.

(2) _____ People in Spain and Greece get their dietary fat mostly from olive oil.

(3) _____ Butter decreases the levels of bad cholesterol in the body.

Graphic Organizer

4 Complete the map using the words from the passage.

	Olive oil	Butter and animal fat
fat	monounsaturated	saturated and (1)_____
type of fat	(2)_____	unhealthier
the risk of heart disease	reduces	(3)_____
the levels of bad cholesterol in the blood	(4)_____	increase

지식
백과

좋은 지방, 나쁜 지방?

지방은 우리 몸에 반드시 필요한 영양소 중 하나이다. 지방은 보통 상온에서 고체 상태인 포화지방과 액체 상태인 불포화지방, 그리고 식품 가공에 사용되는 트랜스지방 등으로 나눌 수 있다. 이 중 포화지방과 트랜스지방은 몸에 과도하게 누적될 경우 각종 성인병의 원인이 되는 등 몸에 해로울 수 있으나, 불포화지방은 몸에 유익한 역할을 한다. 불포화지방은 주로 등푸른 생선이나 콩, 올리브, 견과류 등에 풍부하다.

Welcome to Olive Trees

Fresh
Mediterranean
Restaurant

Olive Trees

5   Welcome!

Our reputation for great food and service has made Olive Trees a one-of-a-kind dining establishment. Since 1997, Olive Trees has truly been the best place <u>to dine</u> in Starr County.

Our goal is to make each visit a delightful and memorable experience. We take

10   great pride in serving our customers fresh, healthy, fast, and affordable Mediterranean food in a friendly atmosphere.

Extraordinarily Fresh and Healthy Food

Check out a wide variety of choices available. They range from appetizers and salads, to BBQ chicken and ribs, steaks, seafood, wraps, and kid's meals.

15   We use healthy, low-fat, low cholesterol, natural ingredients, including the best imported olive oil and low-fat cheese. All our produce and breads are delivered fresh daily.

We also take pride in our consistency of flavor. Our customers come back again because they know they will always get good meals here.

20   ### Authentic European Atmosphere

*Gourmet food is not all that is great about Olive Trees. We are proud of our tradition of serving the best food in an inviting and relaxed atmosphere. Whether you are enjoying a quick lunch with your friends or a dinner with your family, our commitment to fine food and reasonable prices will make your visit to Olive Trees

25   special.

* **gourmet** 미식가의, 고급의

Words

reputation 명 명성   dining 명 식사, 정찬   establishment 명 기관, 시설, 설립   dine 통 식사를 하다
delightful 형 정말 기분 좋은   memorable 형 기억할 만한   affordable 형 (가격이) 알맞은, 감당할 수 있는
atmosphere 명 분위기   extraordinarily 부 엄청나게   appetizer 명 전채, 식욕을 돋우기 위한 것
ingredient 명 재료   consistency 명 일관성   commitment 명 헌신

Text Type

1 The passage is an example of _____.

a. a diary   b. a news article

c. a book report   d. an advertisement

Grammar

2 Which one shows the same function as the underlined to dine?

a. Now is the best time to take a break.

b. Cathy must be upset to hear the news.

c. Chris decided to have salad and pasta.

d. Amy goes to yoga every day to get into shape.

Details

3 Which is NOT mentioned as a good point of Olive Trees?

a. a wide variety of food   b. a relaxed atmosphere

c. cheap prepared food   d. the best imported olive oil

Summary

4 Complete the summary with the words from the passage.

> Since 1997, Olive Trees has been the best Mediterranean _____ to visit in Starr County. It serves Mediterranean food in a friendly _____. It provides a variety of dishes with healthy, low-fat, low-cholesterol, and natural _____. All produce and bread are delivered fresh every day. At Olive Trees, people can enjoy fine food at _____ prices.

지식 백과

슈퍼 푸드, 올리브유

이집트의 람세스 2세는 올리브유를 만병통치약으로 사용했다는 말이 전해질만큼 아주 먼 옛날부터 올리브유의 효용은 널리 알려져 왔다. 최근 올리브유가 심장병 사망률과 몸에 나쁜 콜레스테롤 수치를 낮추고 항산화나 해독 등에도 효과가 있다는 사실이 널리 알려지면서 더욱 많은 사람들이 올리브유를 찾고 있다. 대체로 가공하지 않은 올리브유는 발연점이 낮아서 가급적 튀김 요리 등 고열로 조리를 할 때는 사용하지 않는 것이 좋다고 한다.

○ 올리브의 좋은 점을 동영상으로 만나 보세요. ● Time 2' 54''

A   Unit 01에서 학습한 단어를 생각해 보고, 다음 퍼즐을 완성해 보시오.

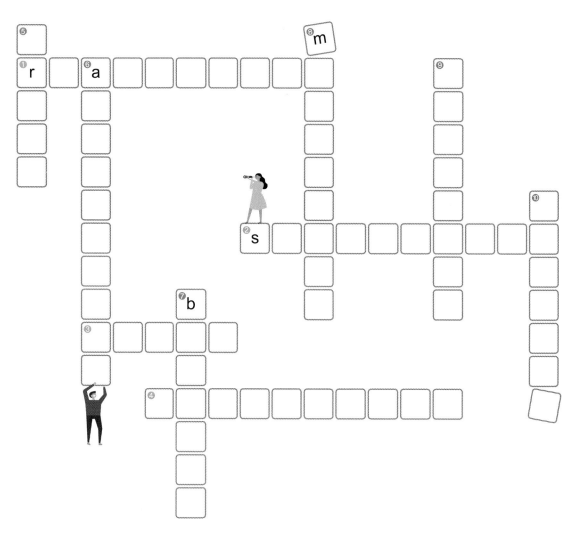

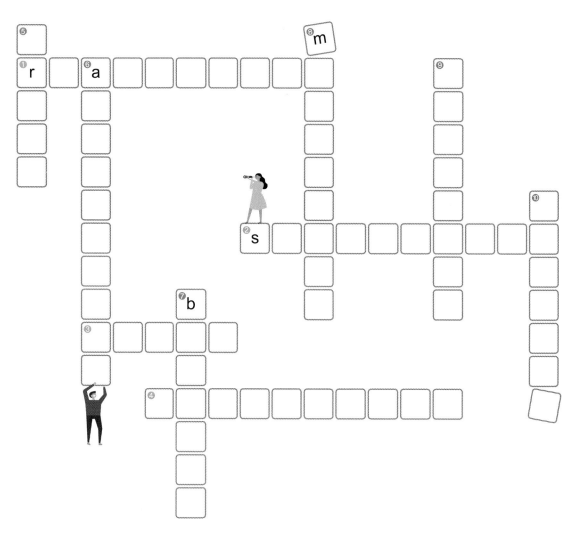 **Across**

① fair and sensible

② to use something instead of another thing

③ to make something less in number or amount

④ 명성을 얻다: gain a _____

 Down

⑤ most important

⑥ priced reasonably

⑦ A _____ means a helpful effect that you get from something.

⑧ worth remembering

⑨ 수입된

⑩ 상품을 배달하다: _____ products

B 다음 [보기]에서 알맞은 말을 골라 문장을 완성하시오.

보기   friendly   benefits   affordable   reduce   ingredient

1 He was delighted that the laptop was _____.

2 The villagers were very _____ to the stranger.

3 Eating an apple a day has great health _____.

4 Exercise can help _____ the risk of heart disease.

5 Flour is the basic _____ of bread along with water and salt.

☀ 생각을 키우는 서술형·수행평가 대비 훈련

C 다음 [보기]에서 알맞은 말을 골라 글을 완성하시오.

　　For my mother's birthday, we decided to take her out for dinner at a nice restaurant. We looked around _____ a restaurant with an inviting and _____ atmosphere and found one called *Olive Trees*. The restaurant serves Mediterranean food which is fresh and _____. This was perfect for Mom because she eats a healthful diet. She consumes small amounts of meat and _____ fat, and she tries to have olive oil every day. Mom had a salad with low-fat cheese and olive oil. She said the dinner was a _____ and delightful experience.

보기   healthy   relaxed   for   memorable   saturated

#*Topic* Sweat, Dehydration & Sports Drinks

엎치락뒤치락 반전을 거듭하며 'palm에 땀을 쥐게' 하는 스포츠 경기를 본 적 있나요? 긴장하거나 놀랐을 때 '식은땀이 나는' 경험을 해본 적은요? 날씨가 더운 것도 아닌데 어째서 자꾸 sweat가 나는 걸까요?

땀이 가진 중요한 기능 중 하나는 몸의 temperature 를 적절한 수준으로 maintain하는 것입니다. 날씨가 덥거나 힘든 운동을 해서 체온이 상승하면 우리 몸에서는 땀이 분비되지요. 이 땀이 evaporate할 때 몸의 열을 빼앗아 가고 그 결과 체온은 average의 상태로 유지되는 거예요. 그런데 박빙의 경기를 보거나 중요한 시험을 앞두고 있을 때처럼 체온과는 상관없이 땀이 produce되는 경우도 있어요. 우리가 긴장하거나 감정적으로 흥분할 때 교감신경계가 stimulate되는데, 이때도 땀이 만들어진답니다. 이렇게 심리 상태에 반응하는 땀을 이용해 거짓말 탐지기를 만들기도 해요. 거짓말을 하는 사람은 심리적으로 불안한 상태이기 때문에 여러 신체 반응이 나타나고 이 중 하나가 손바닥이 damp하게 되는 것이에요. 손바닥이 축축하면 전기가 잘 흐른다는 점을 이용해서 거짓말을 알아채는 것이죠.

어때요? 불쾌한 냄새 때문에 멀리하고만 싶었던 땀이 새롭게 보이나요? 이어지는 글에서는 땀에 대해 자세히 설명해 주고 있어요. 더불어 땀을 많이 흘리면 나타나는 dehydration을 막는 음료 이야기도 있으니, 함께 읽어볼까요?

본문 미리보기 QUIZ

1 땀에서 냄새가 나는 것은 [☐ 염분 ☐ 박테리아] 때문이다. 18쪽에서 확인

2 플로리다 대학교 풋볼팀의 이름은 [☐ Gators ☐ Gatorade] 이다. 20쪽에서 확인

☐ 1	**average** [ǽvəridʒ]	형 평균의, 보통의	평균 키	_____ height
☐ 2	**damp** [dæmp]	형 축축한	축축한 잔디	_____ grass
☐ 3	**dehydration** [dì:haidréiʃən]	명 탈수	탈수를 예방하다	prevent _____
☐ 4	**drenched in**	~으로 흠뻑 젖은	물에 흠뻑 젖은	_____ water
☐ 5	**evaporate** [ivǽpərèit]	동 증발하다	공기 중으로 증발하다	_____ into the air
☐ 6	**fatigue** [fətí:g]	명 피로	피로로 고생하다	suffer from _____
☐ 7	**fluid** [flú:id]	명 유체, 유동체	체액	body _____
☐ 8	**maintain** [meintéin]	동 유지하다	균형을 유지하다	_____ balance
☐ 9	**odorless** [óudərlis]	형 냄새가 없는	무색무취의	colorless and _____
☐ 10	**opponent** [əpóunənt]	명 상대, 반대자	상대를 공격하다	attack the _____
☐ 11	**outplay** [àutpléi]	동 ~보다 더 잘하다	상대측보다 더 잘하다	_____ the opposition
☐ 12	**palm** [pɑ:m]	명 손바닥	손바닥을 들다	hold up a _____
☐ 13	**stimulate** [stímjulèit]	동 자극하다	식욕을 자극하다	_____ appetite
☐ 14	**sweat** [swet]	명 땀	식은땀	a cold _____
☐ 15	**temperature** [témpərətʃər]	명 온도, 체온	낮은 온도	low _____

어휘 자신만만 QUIZ

1 그의 몸은 땀으로 흠뻑 젖는다.

His body is _____ in sweat.

2 그들은 경기의 후반전에서 그들의 모든 상대팀들을 압도했다.

They _____ all their opponents in the second half of the game.

Reading 01

The Science of Sweat

🕐 My Reading Time | Words 218 / 2분 24초

1회 ____분 ____초　2회 ____분 ____초

Cindy is about to make a speech and she notices that her palms are damp with sweat. Fred has just played basketball and his body is drenched in sweat. How can such different activities have the same effect on the body? What is sweat and why do we make it?

5　Sweat is produced in a group of cells called *sweat glands. An average person has about 2.6 million sweat glands in his or her skin. Sweat glands are located over the entire body, except for the lips and nipples. When sweat glands are stimulated by physical heat or emotional stress, a fluid called sweat is produced. Sweat contains mainly water and a small amount of minerals. Sweat itself is odorless. However, bacteria

10　that feed on sweat create an unpleasant odor.

Sweating is our body's main way of cooling itself. When sweat evaporates, it takes heat out of the skin and this helps maintain the body's temperature. (A) Therefore, more sweat is produced when you are hot or doing exercise. (B) Sweat also gets rid of waste from the body. (C) The excessive loss of salt and water can dehydrate the body

15　and cause health problems. (D) So, don't forget to drink enough fluids when you exercise or stay in high temperatures.

* sweat gland 땀샘

Words 　sweat 뗑 땀　palm 뗑 손바닥　damp 혱 축축한　drenched in ~으로 흠뻑 젖은　average 혱 평균의,
보통의　nipple 뗑 젖꼭지　stimulate 통 자극하다　fluid 뗑 유체, 유동체　contain 통 포함하다　odorless
혱 냄새가 없는　evaporate 통 증발하다　temperature 뗑 온도, 체온　dehydrate 통 탈수 상태가 되다

Study Date: /

LINK 실력 향상 WORKBOOK p.6

• Main Idea

1 **Match each paragraph with its main idea.**

(1) Paragraph 1 •

(2) Paragraph 2 •

(3) Paragraph 3 •

• a. People sweat when they do some activities.

• b. Sweating serves useful bodily functions.

• c. Heat or stress stimulates sweat glands to produce sweat.

• Organization

2 **Where would the following sentence best fit?**

However, if you sweat too much, you can get into trouble.

a. (A)   b. (B)   c. (C)   d. (D)

• Inference

3 **Which statement would the writer probably agree with?**

a. Some people never sweat.

b. Sweating too much can be dangerous.

c. Sweating more is helpful when you feel stressed.

d. Sweat glands are located in every part of the body.

• Summary

4 **Complete the summary with the words from the passage.**

Sweat is produced in sweat _____ that are found in most parts of the body. Sweat is mainly made up of water and a few _____. It doesn't smell, but _____ create an odor. Sweating helps the body to _____ down. Sweat also takes _____ out of the body, but sweating too much is dangerous because it can _____ the body.

지식 백과

사막 동물의 땀

땀은 몸의 열을 배출하여 체온을 조절하는 역할을 한다. 뜨거운 사막에 사는 동물들도 땀을 많이 흘릴까? 사막은 기온이 높기도 하지만 매우 건조하고 물이 귀한 곳이므로, 이곳에 사는 동물들의 몸은 수분을 아끼는 방향으로 진화했다. 대표적인 사막 동물인 낙타는 땀을 잘 흘리지 않고 배설물 속에도 수분이 거의 없다.

Reading 02

The Birth of Gatorade

🕐 My Reading Time | Words 225 / 2분 30초

1회 ____분 ____초   2회 ____분 ____초

Gatorade is a well-known sports drink. Many athletes love to drink it to prevent dehydration. How did this famous product get its name? In the early 1960s, a team of researchers at the University of

5　Florida started a project to develop a product which would combat dehydration. Dehydration can cause fatigue and muscle cramps, (A) keep athletes from playing their best. In 1965, the researchers succeeded in developing a drink which would rapidly replace fluid and salt lost

10　during physical activity. They decided to test the new product on 10 members of the University of Florida football team. The name of the team was the Gators, so the product was named "Gatorade."

The football coach recognized the value of Gatorade and had his players drink it. The Gators had a winning season and earned the nickname "the second-half

15　team." They outplayed all their opponents in the second half of the game. When an opposing coach was asked why they lost, he replied, "We didn't have Gatorade. That made the difference."

The rights to Gatorade (B) purchased by the Quaker Oats Company in 1983. Since then, it has been the number one sports drink in the United States. Now

20　Gatorade is produced in 30 different flavors worldwide. It is the official sports drink of many American sports leagues, including the National Football League and the National Basketball Association.

Words

dehydration 몡 탈수　　combat 동 싸우다　　fatigue 몡 피로　　muscle cramp 근육 경련
rapidly 뷘 빠르게　　replace 동 대신하다　　earn 동 얻다, 받다　　outplay 동 ~보다 더 잘하다
opponent 몡 상대, 반대자　　purchase 동 구입하다　　flavor 몡 맛　　worldwide 뷘 전 세계적으로

1 Title

Another title for the passage could be "_____"

a. Who Invented Gatorade?

b. Why Do Athletes Drink Gatorade?

c. How Did Gatorade Become Popular?

d. When Did the Gators Drink Gatorade?

2 Grammar

Write the correct forms of underlined (A) and (B).

(A) → _____   (B) → _____

3 Details

Write T if the statement is true and F if it is false.

(1) _____ Gatorade was developed to help athletes fight dehydration.

(2) _____ Dehydration can cause muscle pain to athletes.

(3) _____ The Gators bought the rights to Gatorade from a company in 1983.

4 Graphic Organizer

Complete the chart using the words from the passage.

Well-known Sports Drink, Gatorade

Who developed it?	A team of researchers at the University of _____.
What was their goal?	To develop a drink that helps fight _____.
Why was it called Gatorade?	The drink was first tested on the football team called the "_____."
Why was it good?	It helped the team play better in the _____ half.
How popular is it?	It is the official drink of many American sports _____.

지식 백과

일사병

땀을 많이 흘린 다음에는 적절하게 수분을 보충해야 한다. 만약 수분 보충이 원활하지 않으면 신체의 온도가 37도~40도 이상으로 오르게 된다. 이런 경우 어지럼증과 함께 구토나 두통 등을 호소하는 일사병 증상이 나타난다. 이러한 증상이 나타나면 즉시 그늘이나 서늘한 곳으로 이동하고 물이나 전해질 음료를 마셔야 한다. 일사병을 예방하기 위해서는 갈증을 느끼기 전에 물이나 이온 음료를 충분히 마셔야 하고, 고온의 환경에서 무리한 활동을 피해야 한다.

▶ 이온 음료에 대해 동영상으로 자세히 알아 보세요. ● Time 2' 00"

Reading Closer

독해의 내공을 키우는 마무리 학습

A Unit 02에서 학습한 단어를 생각해 보고, 다음 퍼즐을 완성해 보시오.

Across

❶ a change that is a result of an event or action

❷ having no smell

❸ 평균적으로: on ______

❹ to play better than

Down

❺ slightly wet

❻ 피로로 고생하다: suffer from ______

❼ 강한 상대: tough ______

❽ the clear liquid that forms on your skin when you are hot or nervous

❾ 공휴일: ______ holiday

❿ whole

B 다음 [보기]에서 알맞은 말을 골라 문장을 완성하시오.

보기	outplay	drenched	fatigue	dehydration	evaporate

1 To avoid _____, you need to drink plenty of water.

2 My new shoes were completely _____ in heavy rain.

3 If you boil water too long, it will _____ and disappear.

4 Despite the long flight, she showed no signs of _____.

5 You have to _____ the other team both physically and mentally.

☀ 생각을 키우는 서술형 · 수행평가 대비 훈련

C 다음 글을 읽고, 밑줄 친 부분 중 어색한 것을 골라 바르게 고치시오.

Sports drinks are very popular among teens. They like drinking the official drink of their ⓐfavorite sports team. But are sports drinks healthy? True, they can help if you sweat. In the case of dehydration, the body has lost ⓑwater and salt. Sports drinks can give them back. However, the drinks also ⓒcontain lots of sugar and colors. Plain water doesn't. To decide what to drink, it is best to remember why sports drinks were developed: to help athletes who sweat ⓓa lot. People who exercise ⓔmore might not need the extra sugar and salt or calories.

_____ → _____

#Topic Map

"100미터 앞에서 좌회전입니다."라고 말하는 똑똑한 내비게이션의 낭랑한 목소리를 들어본 적이 있나요? 요즘은 accurate한 내비게이션 덕분에 traveler들이 낯선 장소에서 길을 헤매는 일이 과거에 비해 많이 줄었어요. 그런데 내비게이션이 없던 시절, 우리 조상들은 어떻게 길을 찾았을까요?

내비게이션이 없었던 과거에 길을 찾기 위해 꼭 필요했던 것이 바로 printed map이었어요. 사람들은 길을 찾기 위해 지도를 봐야했는데, 그 당시 우리나라 지도는 actual한 지형과 다른 내용이 많이 있었어요. 이런 상황을 안타깝게 여긴 사람이 바로 김정호예요. 김정호는 우리나라의 구석구석을 다니며 다양한 지형 정보를 직접 examine하고 목판에 지도를 carve하여 wooden map을 만들었답니다. 이것이 바로 여러분도 잘 아는 '대동여지도'인데, 이것은 한반도의 shoreline과 island, 산, 하천 등을 오늘날의 지도와 거의 일치할 정도로 정확하게 나타냈다고 해요. 게다가 중요한 시설물의 location도 기호를 이용하여 in detail하게 표시했죠.

이후 엄청난 기술 발전 덕분에 예전의 printed된 형태를 벗어나 휴대 전화와 같은 전자기기 안으로 들어온 지도는 우리 삶에 놀라운 convenience를 제공하고 있죠. 지도의 과거와 현재에 관한 이야기를 이어지는 지문에서 좀 더 읽어봐요.

본문 미리보기 QUIZ

1 [□ 그린란드의 이누이트족은] 지도에 축척의 개념을 사용했다.   26쪽에서 확인
    [□ 고대 로마인들은]

2 구글 스트리트 뷰는 사람들의 [□ 사생활을] 침해할 수 있다.   28쪽에서 확인
                              [□ 재산권을]

☐ 1	**accurate** [ǽkjurət]	형 정확한	정확한 정보	_____ information
☐ 2	**carve** [kɑːrv]	동 조각하다, 새기다	호박을 조각하다	_____ pumpkins
☐ 3	**convenience** [kənvíːnjəns]	명 편의, 편리	편의를 제공하다	provide _____
☐ 4	**debate** [dibéit]	명 논쟁, 토론	활기찬 토론	a lively _____
☐ 5	**detail** [ditéil]	명 세부, 상세	세부적으로, 상세하게	in _____
☐ 6	**examine** [igzǽmin]	동 살펴보다	철저하게 살펴보다	thoroughly _____
☐ 7	**island** [áilənd]	명 섬	섬나라	an _____ country
☐ 8	**location** [loukéiʃən]	명 위치	지리적 위치	geographic _____
☐ 9	**marble** [mɑ́ːrbl]	명 대리석	대리석 바닥	a _____ floor
☐ 10	**printed** [príntid]	형 인쇄된	인쇄된 페이지들	_____ pages
☐ 11	**privacy** [práivəsi]	명 사생활	사생활 권리	right to _____
☐ 12	**shoreline** [ʃɔ́ːrlàin]	명 해안선	해안선을 따라	along the _____
☐ 13	**traveler** [trǽvələr]	명 여행자	외국인 여행자	a foreign _____
☐ 14	**violate** [váiəlèit]	동 침해하다	사생활을 침해하다	_____ privacy
☐ 15	**wooden** [wúdn]	형 나무로 된	나무로 된 의자	a _____ chair

어휘 자신만만 QUIZ

1 이누이트 지도는 매우 정확했다고 여겨진다.

It is believed that Inuit maps were very _____.

2 많은 사람들은 이것이 편리함을 준다고 말한다.

Many people say that it offers _____.

For thousands of years, people have traveled to see lands near and far. Today's travelers use printed maps to find their way. How did the travelers of long ago find their way to new places? Believe it or not, many of them also used maps.

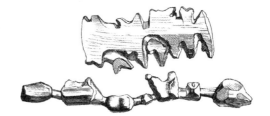

Inuits in Greenland, for example, carved
5 wood to make maps. The map on the right has two pieces of wood. The shorter one shows the shoreline, whereas the longer one shows six islands close to the coast. Inuits used the wooden maps when they traveled at night by kayak. When it was dark, they could read the map by hand to find their
10 way. It is believed that Inuit maps were very accurate.

Ancient Romans added the concept of scale to maps. A map's scale tells the real distance that a distance on a map represents. If an inch on a map stands for 50 miles, cities that are 2 inches apart on the map are about 100 miles apart from each other. In short, scale lets you figure out actual distances by examining a map. A Roman map
15 was usually carved in marble, and it was placed on the wall of a public building so that everyone could use it.

Words

traveler 명 여행자   printed 형 인쇄된   carve 통 조각하다, 새기다   shoreline 명 해안선   island 명 섬
wooden 형 나무로 된   kayak 명 카약   accurate 형 정확한   concept 명 개념   scale 명 축척
represent 통 나타내다   apart 부 떨어져서   examine 통 살펴보다   marble 명 대리석

Purpose

1

What is the purpose of the passage?

a. to talk about personal travel experiences

b. to describe the difficulty of reading maps

c. to present some facts about ancient maps

d. to point out some problems with ancient maps

Details

2

Which of the following is NOT true about Inuit maps?

a. They were made of wood.

b. They could be used in the dark.

c. They were intended for those who traveled by kayak.

d. They were used to tell the real distance between two places.

Reference

3

What does the underlined it refer to?

a. a Roman map

b. marble

c. the wall

d. a public building

Summary

4

Complete the summary with the words from the passage.

Ancient travelers used _____ to find their way, just like modern travelers. Inuits, for instance, used maps made of _____. They could use the maps at _____ because they knew where to go by feeling the map. Ancient Roman maps employed the concept of _____, so people could figure out actual _____ by looking at a map. The Roman maps were placed on the wall of _____ _____.

지식백과

바빌로니아의 점토판 지도

세계에서 가장 오래된 세계 지도는 기원전 약 2300년경에 만들어진 바빌로니아의 점토판 지도이다. 고대 바빌로니아 사람들은 당시 널리 사용하던 소재인 파피루스나 나무가 아닌 점토를 사용하여 지도를 제작했다. 점토판 지도는 점토판 위에 나뭇가지로 그림을 그린 후 이를 단단하게 말려서 만드는 것으로, 이는 파피루스나 나무가 손상되거나 썩기 쉬운 것에 비해 오랜 시간이 지나도 변하지 않는다는 장점이 있다.

Reading 02

Google Street View

Google Street View is a mapping program that provides people views of buildings or streets around the world at eye level. You can see places in detail from the comfort of your home. This is possible because Google Street View uses a large number of car-mounted cameras and displays images of the places you are
5　interested in.

ⓐ Since its launch in 2007, Google Street View has been the subject of hot debate. Many people say that it offers convenience. ⓑ It allows people to visit a location online. ⓒ With a few clicks of your mouse, Google Street View gives you visual information about all kinds of places around the world. ⓓ The biggest
10　problem with Google Street View is the cost. You don't have to travel in person to see them.

On the other hand, there are some people who are deeply concerned. They think that convenience comes at the expense of privacy. What you do in private can be captured by the cameras, and anyone can access this visual information. In
15　theory, it is possible that millions of people are looking into your gardens or windows. It is likely that the information can be misused by people who have no regard for the law. Your privacy can be violated, and even your life may be at risk.

Words　in detail 상세하게　comfort 몡 안락, 편안　display 통 나타내다　debate 몡 논쟁　convenience 몡 편의,

　편리　location 몡 위치　expense 몡 비용, 희생　privacy 몡 사생활　capture 통 (사진으로) 포착하다
access 통 접근하다　visual 혱 시각적인　misuse 통 오용하다　violate 통 침해하다　risk 몡 위험 부담

1 Title

Another title for the passage could be "_____"

a. Is Google Street View Good or Bad?

b. When Did Google Street View Start?

c. Why Do People Use Google Street View?

d. What Information Does Google Street View Offer?

2 Organization

Which sentence does NOT belong?

a. ⓐ   b. ⓑ   c. ⓒ   d. ⓓ

3 Details

Write T if the statement is true and F if it is false.

(1) _____ Google Street View depends on cameras on high mountains.

(2) _____ Google Street View offers images of distant places as well.

(3) _____ Some people are worried that Google Street View may be misused.

4 Graphic Organizer

Complete the map with the words from the passage.

Google Street View

It uses car-mounted (1)_____ and displays images of places at eye level.

Advantages

• You can visit places (2)_____.
• You can get (3)_____ information about places.

Disadvantages

• It can violate (4)_____.
• It can be misused by bad people.

구글 스트리트 뷰, 어떻게 촬영할까?

지식 백과

전 세계 다양한 장소의 이미지를 보여주는 구글 스트리트 뷰는 어떻게 촬영할까? 기본적으로 구글은 360도 촬영이 가능한 카메라를 장착한 차량을 이용하여 스트리트 뷰를 찍는다. 그러나 자동차로 갈 수 없는 곳도 많기 때문에 그 외 다양한 방법도 동원되는데, 사막 지역에서 낙타 등에 카메라를 설치한다거나 눈이 많이 오는 지역에서는 스노우 모빌을 사용하는 경우도 있다. 또한 일본 아키타현에서는 이 지역의 명물인 아키타 견을 활용하여 홍보용 영상을 촬영하기도 했다.

▶ 김정호는 대동여지도를 어떻게 만들었는지 동영상으로 살펴 보세요. ● Time 4' 49''

Reading Closer

A   Unit 03에서 학습한 단어를 생각해 보고, 다음 퍼즐을 완성해 보시오.

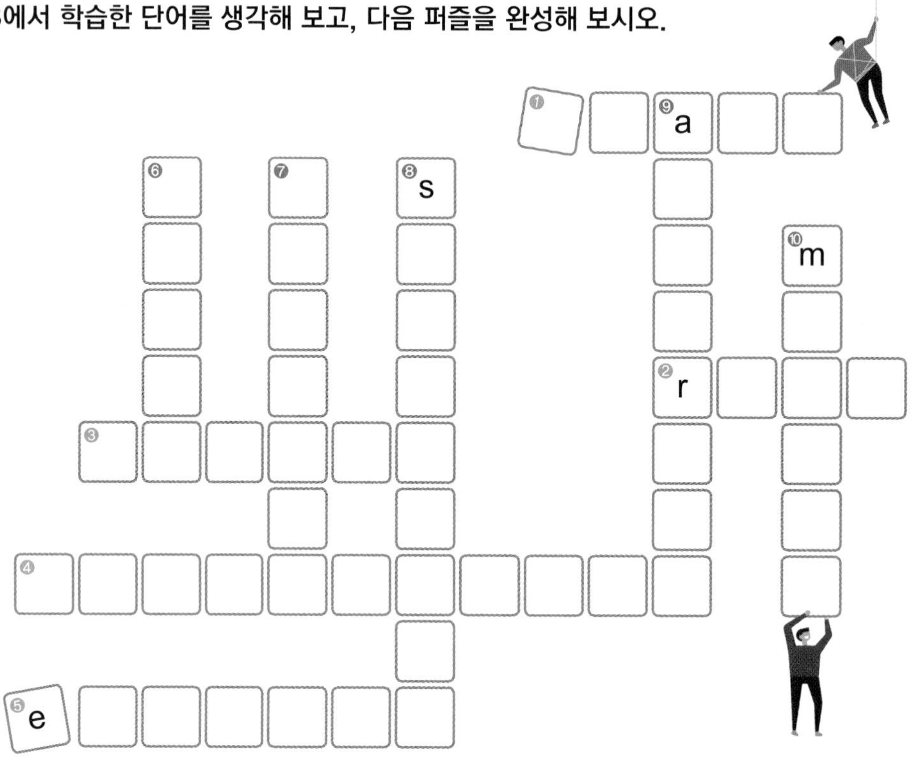

☞ **Across**

❶ 1 : 25,000의 축척: a _____ of 1 : 25,000

❷ 위험하다: be at _____

❸ discussion of a particular issue in which many people take part

❹ 편의를 제공하다: offer _____

❺ to look at something very carefully and in detail

🖐 **Down**

❻ 호박을 조각하다: _____ pumpkins

❼ to break or do something against a law, principle, etc.

❽ the edge of an ocean or a lake

❾ correct and exact in every detail

❿ to use something incorrectly or carelessly

B 다음 [보기]에서 알맞은 말을 골라 문장을 완성하시오.

보기	represent	expense	accurate	violate	misuse

1 The arrows on this map _____ wind direction.

2 The navigation system was not _____, and we got lost.

3 It is important not to _____ other people's rights.

4 He managed to succeed at the _____ of his health.

5 Kids can easily _____ cell phones without parental guidance.

💡 생각을 키우는 서술형 · 수행평가 대비 훈련

C 다음 글을 읽고, 밑줄 친 부분 중 어색한 것을 골라 바르게 고치시오.

My grandfather and I traveled to New York. It ⓐ<u>was</u> a dream of his. When we got there, he said, "Let's find a tourist information center so we can get maps." I said, "We don't need printed maps. I ⓑ<u>have</u> my cellphone." I opened Google Maps. Grandpa wondered how we ⓒ<u>could</u> know distances without seeing the scale of the map. But I showed him how it works. It ⓓ<u>gives</u> all kinds of information. "Look," said Grandpa, "it even tells us the weather!" The trip ⓔ<u>is</u> great. My only concern was: Will Grandpa ever give my phone back?

_____ → _____

생각의 폭을 넓히는 **배경지식 Story**

#*Topic* Silk, Silkworm & Silk Road

여러 가지 옷감 중에서도 silk는 전 세계의 많은 사람이 사랑하는 귀한 material이죠. 그런데 비단이 아주 먼 옛날에도 unbelievably하게 인기 만점이었다는 사실, 알고 있나요?

예로부터 여러 나라에서 비단을 만들었지만 그 중에서도 가장 인기가 있었던 것은 중국의 비단이었어요. 심지어 로마에서도 중국의 비단을 trade했다고 해요! 로마인들에게 중국은 동방의 아득히 먼 나라였지만, 중국의 비단만은 친숙한 것이었죠. 그런데 중국에서 만든 비단이 로마로 가기까지는 여러 desert들과 큰 산맥들을 가로질러야 했어요. 이렇게 먼 여정을 거쳐 도착한 비단은 당연히 매우 값비싸서 주로 로마의 황제나 귀족들의 luxurious한 옷감으로 사용되었죠. 이렇게 중국의 비단이 유럽으로 전해지는 extensive한 network가 바로 실크로드였답니다.

실크로드를 통해 이동한 것은 비단만이 아니었어요. 이 route를 통해서 동양과 서양의 사상, 문물들이 서로 왕래할 수 있었죠. 비단이라는 옷감 하나가 불러일으킨 나비효과가 참 대단하죠? 이어지는 글에서 비단을 만들어내는 insect인 silkworm과 동서양 문물 교류의 route가 되었던 실크로드에 대해 더 자세히 살펴보도록 합시다.

본문 미리보기 QUIZ

1 비단을 만들 수 있는 것은 [☐ 누에 / ☐ 나방] 이다.　　34쪽에서 확인

2 실크로드는 고대 중국 수도인 [☐ 북경 / ☐ 장안] 에서 출발한 무역로였다.　　36쪽에서 확인

☐ 1	**desert** [dézərt]	명 사막	넓은 사막	a broad _____
☐ 2	**extensive** [iksténsiv]	형 광대한	광대한 지식	_____ knowledge
☐ 3	**hatch** [hætʃ]	동 부화하다	알을 부화하다	_____ an egg
☐ 4	**insect** [ínsekt]	명 곤충, 벌레	날고 있는 벌레	a flying _____
☐ 5	**larva** [lά:rvə]	명 애벌레	애벌레로 부화하다	hatch into a _____
☐ 6	**luxurious** [lʌɡʒúːriəs]	형 사치스러운	이 사치스러운 옷감	this _____ cloth
☐ 7	**material** [mətíːəriəl]	명 물질, 재료	가장 강한 물질	the strongest _____
☐ 8	**period** [píːəriəd]	명 마침표	마침표를 찍다	put a _____
☐ 9	**route** [ruːt]	명 통로, 길	우회 경로	an indirect _____
☐ 10	**silk** [silk]	명 비단, 실크	부드러운 비단	soft _____
☐ 11	**silkworm** [sílkwəːrm]	명 누에	누에고치	a _____ cocoon
☐ 12	**thread** [θred]	명 실	튼튼한 실	strong _____
☐ 13	**transform** [trænsfɔ́ːrm]	동 변형시키다	완전히 변형시키다	completely _____
☐ 14	**unbelievably** [ʌnbilíːvəbli]	부 믿을 수 없게도	믿을 수 없게 어리석은	_____ stupid
☐ 15	**vital** [váitl]	형 매우 중요한	매우 중요한 역할	a _____ role

어휘 자신만만 QUIZ

1 당신은 'Bombyx mori'라는 벌레에 대해 들어본 적이 있는가?

Have you ever heard of the _____ *Bombyx mori*?

2 부유한 유럽인들은 이 사치스러운 옷감에 기꺼이 돈을 지불할 의향이 있었다.

Wealthy Europeans were willing to pay for this _____ cloth.

The Life of the Silkworm

My Reading Time | Words 203 / 2분 15초

1회 _____ 분 _____ 초 **2회** _____ 분 _____ 초

Have you ever heard of the insect *Bombyx mori*? The name more commonly used for this insect is "silkworm" because it produces silk. The insect begins its life as a tiny egg. It is as small as the <u>period</u> at the end of this sentence. The egg takes about fourteen days to hatch into a larva. The larva then continuously eats and grows. It only

5 eats the leaves of mulberry trees.

At the next stage of its life, the larva creates a cocoon in about four days. When it is ready to make a cocoon, it has grown to be 10,000 times heavier than when it was an egg. The larva produces one long thread and covers its entire body with it. The cocoon protects the silkworm until it transforms into a moth. This transformation takes about

10 10 days.

If the moth comes out from the cocoon by itself, it will tear most of the thread into small pieces. This makes it difficult to make the best silk. To make higher quality silk, therefore, the cocoons must be boiled before the moths get out. About 3,000 cocoons are needed to make a meter of silk, one of the strongest materials in the world.

Words

insect 명 곤충, 벌레   commonly 부 흔히, 보통   silkworm 명 누에   silk 명 비단, 실크   hatch 동 부화하다
larva 명 애벌레   continuously 부 계속해서, 끊임없이   mulberry 명 뽕나무   cocoon 명 (누에)고치
thread 명 실   transform 동 변화시키다   moth 명 나방   transformation 명 변형, 변태   tear 동 찢다

Study Date: /

• Topic

1 Match each paragraph with an appropriate title.

(1) Paragraph 1 •   • a. The Production of Silk

(2) Paragraph 2 •   • b. The Early Stages of a Silkworm

(3) Paragraph 3 •   • c. The Development of a Cocoon and a Moth

• Words

2 Which has the same meaning as the underlined period?

a. Making quality silk takes a long period of time.

b. That is a question, so you shouldn't use a period.

c. The church was built during the Elizabethan period.

d. The students have Korean history in the last period.

• Details

3 Which is the appropriate time to make silk?

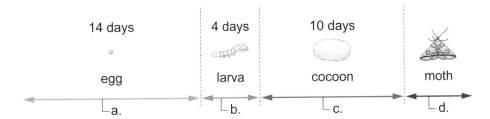

14 days	4 days	10 days	
egg	larva	cocoon	moth
a.	b.	c.	d.

• Summary

4 Complete the summary with the words from the passage.

A silkworm starts out as a very small _____ and turns into a _____ that eats _____ leaves. Then the larva creates a cocoon by producing a _____ and covering itself with it. In about 10 days, the larva turns into a _____, which may come out from the _____ and tear the thread. To produce higher quality silk, therefore, cocoons must be _____ before the moths come out by themselves.

🕐 My Reading Time | Words 218 / 2분 24초

1회 ____ 분 ____ 초   2회 ____ 분 ____ 초

The Silk Road is one of the world's oldest trade routes. Unbelievably, the road is about 2,000 years old. It stretches more than ten thousand kilometers. For more than 14 centuries, the Silk Road was a vital trade route between Asia and Europe.

The Silk Road was not a single route, but an extensive network of trade routes. The road started at Changan, the capital of the ancient Chinese kingdom. ⓐ It continued westward, connecting one oasis to another across Asia's great deserts. ⓑ It went through the Himalayas and split. One branch passed through Russia and was connected to Europe. Another turned south toward India.

The road got ⓒ its name from the Chinese silk trade, which began during the Han Dynasty (206 BC – 220 AD). Wealthy Europeans were willing to pay for this luxurious cloth. Romans considered silk worth ⓓ its weight in gold. Gemstones, perfumes, tea, fine china, and many other items were also carried on this road. However, very few traveled the Silk Road from end to end. Goods were generally passed from middleman to middleman.

The Silk Road was not just a trade route. Knowledge, ideas, and cultures spread through the Silk Road. Trade on the Silk Road was an important factor in the development of the great civilizations of China, India, Egypt, Persia, Arabia, and Rome.

Words

unbelievably 뷔 믿을 수 없게도   stretch 동 뻗다, 뻗치다   vital 형 매우 중요한   trade 명 무역
route 명 통로, 길   extensive 형 광대한   spilt 동 갈라지다   gemstone 명 보석 원석   perfume 명 향수
fine china 정교한 도자기   middleman 명 중간 상인   factor 명 요소   civilization 명 문명

Topic

1 In which paragraphs are the given questions answered?

(1) What items were traded on the Silk Road? → _____

(2) Where did the Silk Road start? → _____

(3) How long is the Silk Road? → _____

Reference

2 Among ⓐ~ⓓ, which refers to a different one?

a. ⓐ   b. ⓑ   c. ⓒ   d. ⓓ

Details

3 Which is true about the Silk Road?

a. It was built in the 14th century.

b. It was a single route connecting Asia to Europe.

c. Gold was the main item traded along the road.

d. It helped the development of many great civilizations.

Graphic Organizer

4 Complete the map with the words from the passage.

	one of the world's (1)_____ trade routes	It is a road that is (2)_____ years old, stretching more than (3)_____ km.
The Silk Road was ...	an extensive (4)_____ of trade routes	Starting from (5)_____, it went through the Himalayas and split, going into Europe and (6)_____.
	a main trade route for (7)_____	Silk and many other items were traded.
	more than a trade route	It contributed to the development of many great (8)_____.

지식 백과

실크로드 개척의 주역, 장건

중국 한나라의 무제는 흉노를 함께 칠 동맹을 맺기 위하여 장건을 대월지에 사신으로 보냈다. 장건은 임무 도중 흉노에 발각되어 10여 년 간 억류되었다가 탈출하여 간신히 대월지에 도착했지만, 동맹을 맺는 데 실패한다. 그러나 그는 대월지에 있으면서 인도와 이집트 등 서역에 대하여 많은 정보를 모을 수 있었고 한나라에 돌아가서 한 무제에게 서역과의 교류를 제안했다. 이러한 노력의 결과로 동·서 간 적극적인 교역이 성사될 수 있었고, 이는 실크로드의 발달로 이어졌다.

Reading Closer

독해의 내공을 키우는 **마무리 학습**

A Unit 04에서 학습한 단어를 생각해 보고, 다음 퍼즐을 완성해 보시오.

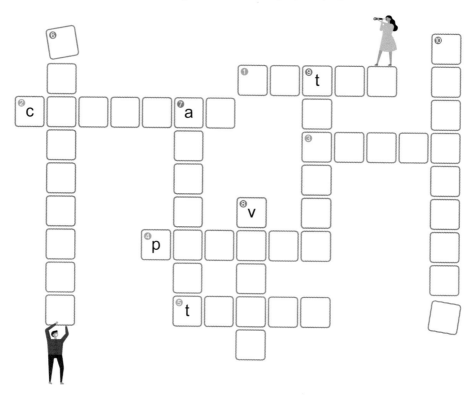

Across

❶ to come out of an egg

❷ Seoul is the _____ of Korea.

❸ 우회 경로: an indirect _____

❹ 마침표를 찍다: put a _____

❺ the buying and selling goods between people or countries

Down

❻ change

❼ belonging to the very distant past

❽ very important

❾ 튼튼한 실: strong _____

❿ 광대한 지식: _____ knowledge

B 다음 [보기]에서 알맞은 말을 골라 문장을 완성하시오.

보기	stretch	hatch	vital	split	transform

1 The hills in the region _____ from east to west.

2 The eggs will _____ after a couple of days.

3 Local artists joined to _____ the old buildings in the area.

4 The committee was _____ into two groups over the issue.

5 Clean water and air are _____ to the health of every living thing on Earth.

☀ 생각을 키우는 서술형 • 수행평가 대비 훈련

C 다음 [보기]에서 알맞은 말을 골라 글을 완성하시오.

Silk has been worn since _____ times, and it is still popular today. The top producer is _____, followed by India. Although people wear and trade silk, some negative ideas about it have spread, too. In Islamic countries, for example, people believe that this _____ and beautiful material is only for women. Those countries are against making silk clothes for men. And, since _____ must be boiled before the moths get out, other people say silk is _____ to animals. They think we should use other high quality, manmade materials instead.

보기	cruel	China	cocoons	ancient	luxurious

생각의 폭을 넓히는 **배경지식 Story**

#Topic Olympic Games & Sponsorship

올림픽은 4년마다 열리는 국제 운동 경기 대회로, **athlete**뿐만 아니라 전 세계 많은 사람들의 관심이 집중되는 축제라고 할 수 있어요. 우리나라는 1988년 서울 올림픽과 **recent** 2018년 평창 동계올림픽, 이렇게 두 번의 **host** 즉, 주최국으로서 올림픽을 개최한 경험이 있어요.

친숙한 체육 행사인 올림픽은 언제 시작된 것일까요? 최초의 올림픽은 제우스 신에게 바치는 축제로 고대 그리스에서 시작되었는데, 올림픽이 열리면 각 도시 국가의 젊은이들이 '올림피아' 라는 곳으로 모였어요. 이들은 레슬링과 같은 올림픽 경기에 **participate**하고 서로 치열하게 **compete**했어요. 전쟁 중이던 도시들도 **at least** 이 기간에는 전쟁을 **entirely** 멈추기로 약속할 만큼 중요한 행사였답니다. 하지만 로마시대에 이르러 올림픽은 더 이상 **maintain**되지 않았고, 이후 1,000년이 넘는 세월 동안 사람들에게서 잊혀졌지요.

이렇게 사라졌던 올림픽이 오늘날 부활하게 된 데는 프랑스의 교육가인 쿠베르텡의 공이 커요. 그는 평화를 **symbolize**하는 고대 올림픽 정신을 다시 살려내면 전 세계에 평화를 가져올 수 있을 것으로 생각했어요. 그래서 그는 평생 올림픽의 발전과 운동 추진에 **dedication**했지요. 그 결과로 1894년에 국제올림픽 위원회(IOC)가 창설되었어요.

그의 노력 덕분에, 우리는 4년마다 멋진 축제를 즐길 수 있는 **opportunity**가 생긴 거죠. 이어지는 글에서 올림픽에 대한 재미있는 이야기를 좀 더 알아볼까요?

본문 미리보기 **QUIZ**

1 올림픽 주최국은 원하는 대로 메달의 [☐ 디자인을 / ☐ 최소 두께를] 정할 수 있다. 42쪽에서 확인

2 TOP 파트너의 권리는 [☐ 4년 동안 / ☐ 8년 동안] 유지된다. 44쪽에서 확인

☐ 1	**advertise** [ǽdvərtàiz]	통 광고하다	제품을 광고하다	_____ products
☐ 2	**athlete** [ǽθliːt]	명 운동선수	위대한 운동선수	a great _____
☐ 3	**compete** [kəmpíːt]	통 경쟁하다	~을 놓고 경쟁하다	_____ for
☐ 4	**confidential** [kὰnfədénʃəl]	형 비밀[기밀]의	기밀 자료	_____ data
☐ 5	**contribute** [kəntríbjuːt]	통 기부하다, 기여하다	돈을 기부하다	_____ money
☐ 6	**dedication** [dèdikéiʃən]	명 헌신	완전한 헌신	total _____
☐ 7	**entirely** [intáiərli]	부 전적으로, 완전히	전적으로 다른	_____ different
☐ 8	**estimate** [éstəmèit]	통 추산하다	공식적으로 추산하다	officially _____
☐ 9	**exclusive** [iksklúːsiv]	형 독점적인	독점적 사용	an _____ use
☐ 10	**extend** [iksténd]	통 연장하다, 확대하다	계약을 연장하다	_____ the contract
☐ 11	**maintain** [meintéin]	통 지속하다, 유지하다	관계를 유지하다	_____ the relationship
☐ 12	**minimum** [mínəməm]	형 최저의, 최소의	최저 임금	_____ wage
☐ 13	**participate** [pɑːrtísəpèit]	통 참가하다	~에 참가하다	_____ in
☐ 14	**revenue** [révənjùː]	명 수익	연간 수익	annual _____
☐ 15	**symbolize** [símbəlàiz]	통 상징하다	행운을 상징하다	_____ good luck

어휘 자신만만 QUIZ

1 그들은 올림픽 메달을 따기 위해 경쟁한다.

They _____ to win Olympic medals.

2 TOP 파트너들은 대개 그들의 후원을 확대한다.

TOP Partners usually _____ their sponsorship.

The True Value of a Medal

Every four years, athletes from around the world come together for the Olympics. They compete to win Olympic medals. Everybody knows that. But do you know who makes the Olympic medals and how much they are worth?

The host country is responsible for producing the medals. This allows each Olympics
5 to have a unique medal. The host country can design the medals as it wishes. However, there are minimum guidelines for the size. Each medal must be at least 60 mm in diameter and 3 mm thick. Some medals for recent Olympics have been larger. In the 2018 Olympics in PyeongChang, for example, the medals were 92.5 mm in diameter.

Olympic gold medals are no longer made of pure gold. They are made up of 92.5%
10 silver and plated with at least 6 grams of gold. This is mostly because it is too expensive to make gold medals out of pure gold. The last Olympic gold medals that were made entirely out of gold _____ in Stockholm, Sweden, in 1912.

So, how much is a gold medal worth? With just 6 grams of gold, it is worth no more than about $600. However, the value of a gold medal doesn't depend on the value
15 of the gold and silver. Winning a gold medal is the dream of every Olympic athlete.

Words

value 명 가치	athlete 명 운동선수	compete 동 경쟁하다	worth 형 ~의 가치가 있는
host 명 (행사의) 주최국	responsible 형 책임이 있는	produce 동 제작하다	unique 형 독특한
minimum 형 최저의, 최소한의	guideline 명 가이드라인, 지침	at least 적어도, 최소한	diameter 명 지름
pure 형 순수한	plate 동 도금하다	entirely 부 전적으로, 완전히	depend on ~에 달려 있다

1

— Title

Match Paragraph 2, 3, and 4 with appropriate titles.

(1) Paragraph 2 •   • a. The Makeup of Olympic Gold Medals

(2) Paragraph 3 •   • b. The Value of Olympic Gold Medals

(3) Paragraph 4 •   • c. The Size and Design of Olympic Medals

2

— Grammar

Which is the best choice for the blank?

a. awarded   b. are awarded

c. was awarded   d. were awarded

3

— Details

Write T if the statement is true and F if it is false.

(1) _____   Olympic medals are made by the host country.

(2) _____   The medals for the 2018 Olympics were about one and half times as long as the guideline requires in diameter.

(3) _____   Pure gold is used in all Olympic gold medals.

4

— Graphic Organizer

Complete the map using the words from the passage.

Olympic Medals

Who?	• The _____ _____ is responsible for their production and design. – They must be at least 60 mm in _____ and _____ mm thick. – Today's gold medals contain 92.5% _____ and 6 grams of gold.
How much?	• With 6 grams of gold, they are worth about _____ each. • They are treasured by Olympic _____.

Olympic Sponsorship

My Reading Time | Words 232 / 2분 33초
1회 ____ 분 ____ 초   2회 ____ 분 ____ 초

Participating in the Olympic Games is a dream for many athletes. And for many companies, too. As one of the most popular and most watched events in the world, the Olympic Games provide great business opportunities for companies. They have become one of the best places for advertising and marketing.

5 The Olympic Games symbolize youthful energy, dedication and high achievement, and companies love to be associated with these ideals. So, many companies are willing to pay lots of money to be a sponsor. Sponsors contribute cash, products and services. _____, sponsors receive the exclusive right to use the Olympic images in their advertising and promotions. Without support from the 10 sponsors, the Olympic Games cannot happen. Revenue on sponsorship makes up more than 40% of Olympic revenue.

There are different levels of sponsorship. On the highest level is the IOC's TOP (The Olympic Partners) Programme. TOP partners must be able to provide not only cash but also direct support and know-how for 15 the Games. How much is needed to be a TOP Partner is confidential, but it is estimated at much more than 50 million dollars for the four-year right.

Does Olympic sponsorship really increase brand awareness and product sales? Many companies seem 20 to believe so. TOP partners usually extend their sponsorship and maintain their relationship with the Olympic Games. For example, the Coca-Cola Company has supported every Olympic Games since 1928.

Words

participate 동 참가하다   opportunity 명 기회   advertise 동 광고하다   symbolize 동 상징하다
dedication 명 헌신   achievement 명 성취   associate with ~와 결부[연관]짓다   ideal 명 이상
contribute 동 기부하다, 기여하다   receive 동 받다   exclusive 형 독점적인   promotion 명 홍보
revenue 명 수익, 수입   confidential 형 비밀[기밀]의   estimate 동 추산하다   extend 동 연장하다, 확대하다

1 • Main Idea

What is the main idea of the passage?

a. The Olympic Games should not rely on money from sponsors.

b. Thanks to the support of sponsors, the Olympic Games can be held.

c. Many companies received economic benefits from the TOP Programme.

d. Many companies use the Olympic Games as a chance for advertising and marketing.

2 • Linking

Which is the best choice for the blank?

a. For example

b. In return

c. In spite of it

d. Unfortunately

3 • Details

Complete the statements with the words from the passage.

(1) Only sponsors can use the Olympic _____ in their promotions.

(2) Many companies believe Olympic sponsorship increases brand awareness and

_____ _____ .

4 • Summary

Complete the summary with the words from the passage.

> The Olympic Games provide great _____ opportunities for companies.
> Many companies are willing to be a _____ of the Olympic Games.
> Sponsors have to provide money, _____ and services. Then they have
> the _____ right to use the Olympic images in their advertising and
> promotions. TOP partners must be able to provide direct support and
> _____ as well as cash.

스포츠 산업의 전문 인력, 스포츠 마케터

스포츠 마케터는 스포츠 기업이 대중에게 회사의 이름을 알리고, 긍정적인 이미지를 심어줄 수 있도록 마케팅 업무를 수행하며 스포츠와 관련된 각종 행사의 지원, 스포츠 용품 판매, 스포츠 선수의 관리 등을 맡아 한다. 스포츠 마케터가 되는 데 학력이나 전공 등의 제한은 없지만 업무 수행을 위해서는 마케팅에 대한 기본 지식, 어학 실력, 커뮤니케이션 능력 등이 필요하다. 하지만 무엇보다 중요한 것은 스포츠를 좋아하고 즐기는 열정이다.

지식백과

A   Unit 05에서 학습한 단어를 생각해 보고, 다음 퍼즐을 완성해 보시오.

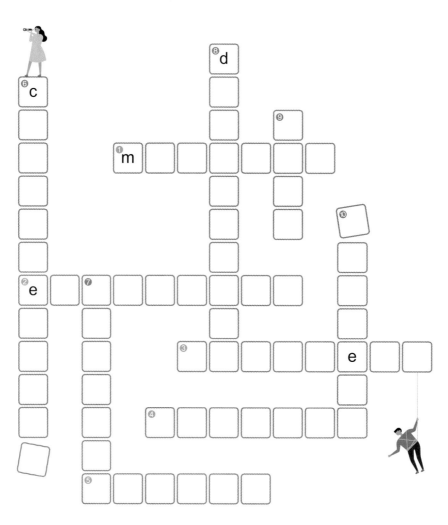

Across

❶ the opposite of maximum

❷ not shared with anyone else

❸ a similar word of completely

❹ to get something that is sent to you

❺ Could you _____ the deadline?

   (마감 기한을 연장해 주실 수 있나요?)

Down

❻ meant to be kept secret

❼ to try to be better than other people

❽ 완전한 헌신: total _____

❾ 순금: _____ gold

❿ a person who is trained and highly skilled in sports

B 다음 [보기]에서 알맞은 말을 골라 문장을 완성하시오.

> **보기**   revenue   symbolize   estimate   worth   participate

1 I _____ his age at about 40.

2 The painting is _____ more than a million dollars.

3 Young athletes hope to _____ in the Olympic Games.

4 The company is looking for new sources of _____.

5 The five rings on the Olympic flag _____ the five continents.

🔆 **생각을 키우는 서술형·수행평가 대비 훈련**

C 다음 글을 읽고, 밑줄 친 부분 중 어색한 것을 골라 바르게 고치시오.

> Olympic gold medals are not made of pure gold, but athletes still want to ⓐwin them. Not long ago, one dedicated U.S. gymnast earned four of them! Her name is Simone Biles. In 2016, Simone Biles set an American record for winning the most gold medals in women's *gymnastics in a single Olympic Games. These medals gave her ⓑfewer opportunities. Many companies became ⓒaware of her energy and high achievement. Naturally, they wanted to be associated with her ⓓimage. They wanted to increase their brand awareness and sales. Today, Biles shows several famous ⓔsponsors on her website.
>
> * gymnastics 체조

_____ → _____

#Topic Internet & Technology

인터넷이 없는 세상, 상상해 본 적 있나요? 우리는 매일 다양한 전자 device를 사용하여 웹 사이트에 접속하고 정보를 browse하는 데 적지 않은 시간을 보내죠. 인터넷과 관련된 기술과 서비스는 이제 우리 삶에 undoubtedly 필수적인 것이 되었어요.

우리가 인터넷을 쉽게 사용할 수 있도록 가장 큰 contribution을 한 사람이 바로 영국의 컴퓨터 공학자 Tim Berners-Lee예요. 그는 우리가 인터넷 주소창에 입력하는 "WWW", 즉 월드 와이드 웹이라는 tool을 개발해서 전 세계 사람들이 웹을 통해 데이터에 접근하는 것을 가능하게 해 주었어요. 심지어 그는 이런 invention을 무료로 개방해서 인터넷이 빠르게 발전할 수 있도록 했죠. 정말 대단하죠? 그는 모든 사람이 인터넷에 connect할 권리가 있다고 믿었어요.

2009년에 Tim Berners-Lee는 웹 브라우저와 관련된 흥미로운 이야기를 밝히기도 했어요. 바로 인터넷 주소를 organize하는 'https://'에서 뒤에 있는 두 개의 슬래쉬 (//)가 사실 specific한 의미를 indicate하지 않는다는 것이죠. 그는 많은 사람들이 이것 때문에 시간과 잉크, 종이를 낭비하게 되어서 미안하다고 했다는군요. 하지만 인터넷이 우리 삶을 얼마나 편리하게 해주었는지를 생각한다면 이 정도는 큰 불편이 아니겠죠? 재미있는 인터넷의 세계, 이어지는 지문에서 좀 더 알아봐요.

본문 미리보기 QUIZ

1 인터넷은 Tim Berners-Lee가 [☐ 1955년 / ☐ 1989년] 에 발명했다. 50쪽에서 확인

2 인터넷 웹사이트나 파일 주소를 나타내는 용어는 [☐ URL / ☐ MVP] 이다. 52쪽에서 확인

☐ 1	**benefit** [bénəfit]	통 득을 보다	~으로 득을 보다	_____ from
☐ 2	**browse** [brauz]	통 열람하다, 검색하다	인터넷을 검색하다	_____ the Internet
☐ 3	**contribution** [kὰntrəbjúːʃən]	명 기여	긍정적인 기여	a positive _____
☐ 4	**device** [diváis]	명 장치	의료 장치	a medical _____
☐ 5	**identify** [aidéntəfài]	통 확인하다, 알아보다	지문을 식별하다	_____ a fingerprint
☐ 6	**indicate** [índikèit]	통 나타내다	유형을 나타내다	_____ the type
☐ 7	**invention** [invénʃən]	명 발명(품)	놀라운 발명품	an amazing _____
☐ 8	**organize** [ɔ́ːrgənàiz]	통 구성하다	효과적으로 구성하다	effectively _____
☐ 9	**particular** [pərtíkjulər]	형 특정한	특정한 순간	a _____ moment
☐ 10	**request** [rikwést]	명 요청	정중한 요청	a polite _____
☐ 11	**separate** [sépərèit]	통 분리하다, 나누다	역할을 분리하다	_____ roles
☐ 12	**specific** [spisífik]	형 구체적인, 특정한	특정한 목적	a _____ purpose
☐ 13	**tool** [tuːl]	명 도구	유용한 도구	a useful _____
☐ 14	**translate** [trænsléit]	통 번역하다	정확하게 번역하다	correctly _____
☐ 15	**undoubtedly** [ʌndáutidli]	부 의심할 바 없이	확실히 틀렸다	_____ wrong

어휘 자신만만 QUIZ

1 그는 여전히 자신의 발명품으로 모든 사람들이 혜택을 받기를 원한다.

He still wants everyone to _____ from his invention.

2 URL은 인터넷상의 특정한 웹 사이트 혹은 파일의 주소이다.

A URL is the address of a _____ website or a file on the Internet.

Who Invented the WWW?

🕐 My Reading Time I Words 220 / 2분 24초

1회 _____ 분 _____ 초   **2회** _____ 분 _____ 초

Most Internet addresses begin with WWW, the initials for the World Wide Web. Some people think that the World Wide Web is the same thing as the Internet. But this isn't true. The Internet is a large network of computers around the world. It connects countless computers in different countries. The World Wide Web, _____, is a tool that allows people to organize, link, and browse pages on the Internet.

Tim Berners-Lee invented this powerful tool in 1989. He was born in London in 1955 and studied physics at Oxford University. While working in a physics laboratory called CERN in Geneva, Switzerland, he felt the need to develop a tool to share information over the Internet. Thanks to his invention, anyone can get to the huge amount of information on the Internet quickly and easily.

His work is regarded by some as being as important as Gutenberg's printing press. Undoubtedly, he could have been rich or famous. But he didn't want the spotlight or money. In fact, he has fought hard to make sure that nobody owns the World Wide Web. He still wants everyone to benefit from his invention. Thus, the tool is free for all, and it will remain so. Berners-Lee was knighted by Queen Elizabeth II in 2004 for his contribution to the world.

Words

invent 통 발명하다   address 명 주소   initial 명 머리글자   connect 통 연결[접속]하다   countless 형 셀 수 없이 많은   tool 명 도구   organize 통 구성하다   link 통 연결[접속]하다   browse 통 열람하다, 검색하다   physics 명 물리학   laboratory 명 실험실   develop 통 개발하다   huge 형 엄청난   undoubtedly 부 의심할 여지 없이   spotlight 명 (세간의) 주목, 관심   benefit 통 득을 보다   contribution 명 공헌, 기여

Main Idea

1

What is the main idea of the passage?

a. Anyone can access the information on the Internet.

b. The World Wide Web allows people to browse webpages.

c. Tim Berners-Lee's invention is as important as Gutenberg's printing press.

d. The invention of the World Wide Web by Tim Berners-Lee helped many people around the world.

Linking

2

Which is the best choice for the blank?

a. therefore
b. otherwise
c. for example
d. on the other hand

Details

3

Which is true about Tim Berners-Lee?

a. He worked in a laboratory in Switzerland.

b. He invented the World Wide Web in 1955.

c. He became rich after inventing the World Wide Web.

d. He became a knight in 1989.

Summary

4

Complete the summary with the words from the passage.

The World Wide Web is a tool that allows people to _____, link, and browse webpages. It was invented by Tim Berners-Lee in _____. His invention is considered as important as Gutenberg's _____ _____. However, he didn't want to become famous or _____ from his invention. He just wanted everyone to benefit from his work. The World Wide Web is and will remain _____ for all.

Easy Internet Terms

A **Web browser** is a piece of software that enables us to read webpages. It translates the coding language (HTML) of the World Wide Web into graphic form and displays webpages. Thanks to web browsers, we can enjoy web surfing by simply clicking, without having to know a coding language.

5　　A **URL** is the address of a specific website or a file on the Internet. The first part of a URL indicates the type of resource. Most URLs begin with "http." The second part of a URL contains the address of the computer and path to the file. For example, in "http://www.enet.com/Content/Reports/index.html," "www.enet. com" is the address or domain name of the host computer and "/Content/Reports/

10　index.html" is _____ .

An **IP address** is a code made up of numbers which identifies a particular device on the Internet. Every device, such as a computer or a printer, must have an IP address in order to communicate with other devices on the Internet. It shows where the device is. An IP address consists of four sets of numbers from 0 to 255,

15　each separated by one dot.

DNS is the system that translates domain names into IP addresses. When you type in "http://www.google.com," the computer sends a request to the nearest DNS server,

20　which finds the correct IP address for "google.com." Without DNS, we would have

to remember the IP address of every site we want to visit.

Purpose

1 **What is the purpose of the passage?**

a. to explain some basic terms from the Internet

b. to explain how to create a domain name on the Internet

c. to show how to find the site you want to visit on the Internet

d. to make clear the difference between an IP address and a URL

Inference

2 **Which is the best choice for the blank?**

a. the path to the file

b. the type of resource

c. the address of the computer

d. the domain name of the host computer

Details

3 **According to the passage, which might be a proper IP address?**

a. 211.43.138   b. 127.216.187   c. 2.255.255.0   d. 136.243.349.221

Graphic Organizer

4 **Complete the map using the words from the passage.**

Internet Terms	Web browser	program that translates HTML code and _____ webpages
	URL	address of a specific website, consisting of two parts - the first part shows the type of _____ and the second part indicates the address of the computer and _____ to the file
	IP address	code of _____ sets of numbers that identifies a particular _____ on the internet
	DNS	system that translates _____ names into IP addresses

도메인 사냥꾼을 잡아라

지식백과

'(남의 땅을) 불법 점유하다'라는 뜻의 영어 단어 squat에서 유래한 '사이버스쿼팅(cyber-squatting)'은 판매를 목적으로 도메인을 선점하고 있다가 관련 기업에게 비싼 가격으로 도메인을 되파는 것을 말한다. '도메인 사냥꾼'들은 유명 브랜드, 유명인, 심지어 나라 이름까지 선점하기도 한다. 우리나라에서는 '인터넷주소자원관리법'을 제정하여 판매 또는 영업 방해를 목적으로 도메인을 선점하는 행위를 금지하고 있다.

독해의 내공을 키우는 **마무리 학습**

A   Unit 06에서 학습한 단어를 생각해 보고, 다음 퍼즐을 완성해 보시오.

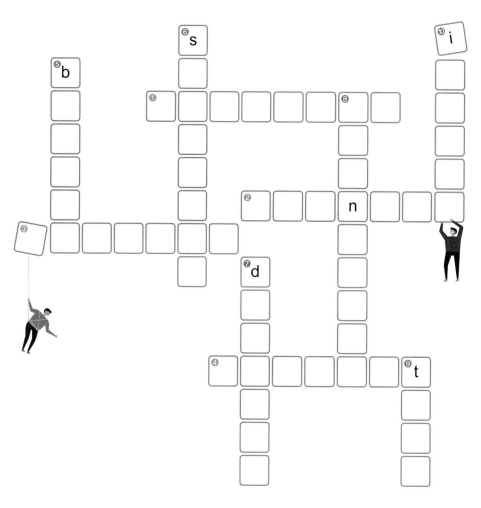

👉 **Across**

❶ to divide or cause to move apart

❷ 인터넷에 접속하다: _____ to the Internet

❸ 그 거래로 이득을 보다: _____ from the deal

❹ 정중한 요청: a polite _____

👇 **Down**

❺ to scan through information on a computer

❻ 특정한 목적: a _____ purpose

❼ 제품을 개발하다: _____ a product

❽ _____ a Korean novel into French
 (한글 소설을 프랑스어로 번역하다)

❾ something that you hold in your hand and use for a particular task

❿ to design or think of something that has not existed before

B 다음 [보기]에서 알맞은 말을 골라 문장을 완성하시오.

보기	browse	translate	regard	indicate	contain

1 These signs _____ the speed limit.

2 Students _____ him as a great scholar.

3 These documents _____ details of the event.

4 This app is able to _____ between different languages.

5 Many people _____ through websites from their cellphones.

☀ 생각을 키우는 서술형 · 수행평가 대비 훈련

C 다음 글을 읽고, 밑줄 친 부분 중 어색한 것을 골라 바르게 고치시오.

My mom remembers life before the World Wide Web was invented. She said that when she ⓐ was in college long ago, she took a course on computers. The teacher introduced a coding language ⓑ making up of numbers and shared information about how devices worked. "It seemed terribly complicated," she said. "There was no simple clicking like today." These days, however, my mom loves computers. She ⓒ surfs the Internet and visits many webpages. "What do you ⓓ think of Berners-Lee?" I asked her. She said, "He is a genius. Everyone ⓔ benefits from his invention!"

_____ → _____

생각의 폭을 넓히는 **배경지식 Story**

#*Topic* Halloween & Folklore

Trick
or
Treat

매년 10월 31일, 어린이들이 유령, 마녀, 괴물 등의 costume을 입고 집집마다 돌아다니며 사탕이나 과자를 요구하며 celebrate하는 서양 custom이 무엇인지 아나요? 바로 핼러윈이에요. 원래 핼러윈은 서양에서 originate한 명절이지만 어느덧 우리나라에서도 많은 사람들에게 익숙해졌지요.

우리나라에도 핼러윈과 비슷한 날이 있답니다. '동지'라는 절기의 이름을 들어본 적이 있을 거예요. 일 년 중 낮이 가장 짧고 그 opposite으로 밤이 가장 긴 날을 '동지'라고 해요. 이날 이후로는 낮이 밤보다 조금씩 더 길어지기 시작하는데, 사람들은 이것을 해가 다시 부활하는 것으로 여겨서 동지를 일 년의 시작으로 간주하고 해를 devide하기도 했어요. 또 동짓날 긴 밤 동안 마을을 wander하는 evil spirit을 쫓기 위해 집 주위에 팥을 놓아두거나 팥죽을 쑤어 먹기도 했지요. 귀신이 붉은 팥을 무서워한다고 생각했기 때문이에요.

어때요, 우리나라의 동지와 핼러윈이 비슷하다고 생각되나요? 악령을 turn away하고 복을 빌고 싶은 마음은 문화권에 상관없이 누구에게나 있는 것 같아요. 이어지는 글에서 핼러윈의 tradition이 어떻게 시작되었는지, 그리고 그에 관한 재미있는 folklore에 대해 좀 더 알아봅시다.

본문 미리보기 QUIZ

1 핼러윈의 복장은 [☐ 켈트족 / ☐ 어린이] 축제에서 유래되었다. 58쪽에서 확인

2 Stingy Jack은 [☐ 순무 / ☐ 호박] 속에 잉걸불을 넣고 돌아다닌다. 60쪽에서 확인

☐ 1 **celebrate** [séləbrèit] 동 기념하다, 축하하다 | 공식적으로 기념하다 | officially _____

☐ 2 **costume** [kástuːm] 명 의상 | 민속 의상 | a national _____

☐ 3 **custom** [kʌ́stəm] 명 관습, 풍습 | 흔한 관습 | a common _____

☐ 4 **evil spirit** 사악한 영혼, 악령 | 악령을 없애다 | get rid of an _____

☐ 5 **folklore** [fóuklɔ̀ːr] 명 민속, 민담 | 중국 민담 | Chinese _____

☐ 6 **haunt** [hɔːnt] 동 (유령이) 출몰하다 | (유령이) 집에 출몰하다 | _____ the house

☐ 7 **hollow** [hálou] 형 (속이) 빈 | (속이) 빈 나무 | a _____ tree

☐ 8 **holy** [hóuli] 형 성스러운 | 신성한 동물 | a _____ animal

☐ 9 **opposite** [ápəzit] 형 다른 편의, ~의 맞은편의 | 반대 방향 | the _____ direction

☐ 10 **originate** [ərídʒənèit] 동 비롯되다, 유래하다 | ~에서 유래하다 | _____ from

☐ 11 **soot** [suːt] 명 그을음, 검댕 | 그을음에 덮인 | covered with _____

☐ 12 **toss** [tɔːs] 동 던지다 | 공을 던지다 | _____ a ball

☐ 13 **treat** [triːt] 명 특별한 것 동 대하다, 대접하다 | 우리의 생일 선물 | our birthday _____

☐ 14 **turn away** 쫓아 버리다 | 기자들을 쫓아 버리다 | _____ reporters

☐ 15 **wander** [wándər] 동 돌아다니다, 헤매다 | 거리를 돌아다니다 | _____ the streets

어휘 자신만만 QUIZ

1 전 세계의 사람들은 의상을 입고 사탕을 가지고 핼러윈을 기념한다.

People around the world _____ Halloween with costumes and candy.

2 악마는 그에게 지옥의 화염에서 잉걸불을 던졌다.

The Devil _____ him an ember from the flames of Hell.

History of Halloween

🕐 My Reading Time | Words 231 / 2분 33초

1회 ____ 분 ____ 초   **2회** ____ 분 ____ 초

On October 31, people around the world celebrate Halloween with costumes and candy. The name "Halloween" came from "All Hallows Eve," which meant the night before All Hallows Day. All Hallows Day was a holy day in *Christianity honoring the saints and other people who had died for their religion.

5　　Some customs of Halloween such as costumes and gifts, however, originated from the Celtic festival of Samhain. The Celts divided the year into halves: the light half and the dark half. The light half was the time when the days were longer and the dark half was the opposite. Samhain was held on the day when the light half ended and the dark half began. The Celts believed that the souls of the recently dead could walk the

10　earth on this night. People didn't want to be haunted by unhappy ghosts. So they would parade to the outskirts of their villages and leave sweet treats. They hoped that the dead would follow the parade and not cause them any harm. To confuse evil spirits, they would often paint their faces with soot and wear costumes made with straw and animal skins.

15　These days, Halloween is not usually considered a religious holiday. It is primarily a fun day for children. Children dress up in costumes as the Celts did a long time ago. However, they _____ .

* **Christianity** 기독교

Words

celebrate 통 기념하다, 축하하다　　costume 명 의상　　holy 형 성스러운　　honor 명 명예 통 존경하다　　saint 명 성인　　religion 명 종교　　custom 명 관습　　originate 통 비롯되다, 유래하다　　opposite 형 다른 편의, ~의 맞은편의　　soul 명 영혼　　haunt 통 (유령이) ~에 나타나다, 출몰하다　　parade 통 행진하다　　outskirt 명 교외, 변두리　　treat 명 특별한 것　　soot 명 그을음, 검댕　　primarily 부 주로

Topic

1 This passage is mainly about _____.

a. the origin of Halloween

b. the fun of Halloween parades

c. how to make Halloween costumes

d. the difference between Halloween and Samhain

Reference

2 What does the underlined the opposite mean?

→ The time when _____ than the days

Inference

3 Which is the best choice for the blank?

a. don't believe in God anymore

b. parade to the outskirts of their village

c. don't worry too much about evil spirits

d. celebrate the beginning of the dark half

Graphic Organizer

4 Complete the map using the words from the passage.

Halloween

Its name originated from

Some of its customs originated from

All Hallows Day
• It is a holy day in Christianity honoring the (1)_____ and people who had died for their (2)_____.

Samhain
• It is the (3)_____ festival held on the day when the (4)_____ half began. • People would parade, (5)_____ sweets, and wear (6)_____.

지식백과

과자를 주지 않으면 장난칠 거예요!(Trick or treat!)

매년 10월 31일, 핼러윈이 되면 미국이나 유럽의 어린이들은 유령으로 분장을 하고 집마다 돌아다니면서 "Trick or treat!"라고 외친다. 맛있는 것을 주지 않으면 장난을 치겠다는 의미이다. 어른들은 과자나 사탕은 준비해 아이들을 맞이하는데, 문 앞에는 호박 속을 파내어 도깨비 얼굴 모양을 만들고 그 안에 촛불을 밝혀 놓은 잭오랜턴을 놓는다. 어떤 사람들은 자선활동 등을 하며 이날을 뜻깊게 보내기도 한다.

▶ 핼러윈 데이의 문화를 동영상으로 만나 보세요. ⏱ Time 3' 10"

Stingy Jack and the Devil

According to Irish folklore, there once lived a man named Stingy Jack. He was a miserable old drunk who liked to play tricks on everybody. One day, he tricked the Devil into climbing an apple tree and then planted crosses around the tree. The Devil couldn't get down. Jack told the Devil he would let him down

5   (A) ⌈if / unless⌉ he promised not to take his soul when he died. When the Devil agreed, Jack removed all the crosses and let the Devil down.

Many years later, ⓐ Jack died. He went to Heaven but was turned away because he had led a worthless life. So, then ⓑ he went down to Hell. However, the Devil kept ⓒ his promise and didn't let him in. Jack now had nowhere to go. He asked

10 the Devil how he could see where to go with no light. The Devil tossed ⓓ him an *ember from the flames of Hell. Jack put it inside a hollowed turnip, which he always carried with him, and began wandering to find a resting place. He became known as "Jack of the Lantern."

On All Hallows Eve, the Irish

15 hollowed out turnips and placed lights inside them. They left a jack-o' lantern on their doorsteps to keep Jack and other evil spirits away. When the tradition (B) ⌈brought /

20 was brought⌉ to America, pumpkins replaced turnips.

* **ember** 잉걸불, 타다 남은 불

Words

folklore 몡 민속, 민담   miserable 휑 비열한, 못된, 비참한   cross 몡 십자가   soul 몡 영혼   remove 동 제거하다   worthless 휑 가치가 없는   Hell 몡 지옥   toss 동 던지다   ember 몡 잉걸불   flame 몡 화염   hollow 휑 (속이) 빈   turnip 몡 순무   wander 동 돌아다니다, 헤매다   lantern 몡 랜턴, 손전등   doorstep 몡 문간   evil spirit 악령, 귀신   tradition 몡 전통   pumpkin 몡 호박   replace 동 대체하다

1 • Title

Another title for the passage could be "_____."

a. How Jack Tricked the Devil

b. How the Tradition of Jack-O' Lanterns Began

c. How a Jack-O' Lantern Kept Evil Spirits Away

d. Advantages of Planting Pumpkins Instead of Turnips

2 • Grammar

Choose the words that fit in boxes (A) and (B).

(A)	(B)		(A)	(B)
a. if	⋯⋯ brought		b. unless	⋯⋯ brought
c. if	⋯⋯ was brought		d. unless	⋯⋯ was brought

3 • Details

Which one does NOT refer to the same thing?

a. ⓐ   b. ⓑ   c. ⓒ   d. ⓓ

4 • Summary

Complete the summary with the words from the passage.

There once lived an old _____ called Stingy Jack. One day, he tricked the Devil and made him promise not to take his _____ when he died. Jack died. He was not welcomed in _____. He couldn't enter Hell either, because the Devil kept his _____. So, he began wandering for a _____ place, using a jack-o' lantern for light. Later the Irish left a jack-o' lantern on their _____ on All Hallows Eve.

지식백과

사과 건지기(Apple Bobbing) 놀이

핼러윈에 아이들이 즐겨 하는 놀이 중에 '사과 건지기(Apple Bobbing)'가 있다. 집마다 돌아다니며 간식을 받은 아이들은 모여서 파티를 여는데, 이때 물을 채운 대야에 사과를 띄운 다음 손을 쓰지 않고 입으로만 그것을 건지는 놀이를 한다. 사과는 잭오랜턴의 이야기에 등장하는 핼러윈의 상징인 동시에 로마 신화에 등장하는 과일의 여신 포모나의 상징이기도 하다.

A   Unit 07에서 학습한 단어를 생각해 보고, 다음 퍼즐을 완성해 보시오.

Across

❶ 순무

❷ the clothes worn to look like somebody else

❸ an accepted way of behaving in a society or time

❹ to begin for the first time in a particular place or situation

❺ 크리스마스를 기념하다: _____ Christmas

❻ to walk slowly around without any a clear purpose

Down

❼ 고요한 밤, 거룩한 밤: silent night, _____ night

❽ 비참한 삶: a _____ life

❾ 공을 던지다: _____ a ball

❿ The _____ of 'high' is 'low.'
   ('높은'의 반대는 '낮은'이다.)

B 다음 [보기]에서 알맞은 말을 골라 문장을 완성하시오.

| 보기 | wander | treat | tradition | trick | hollow |

1 Fortune cookies are _____ inside.

2 We should not _____ around the park at night.

3 I was upset when I found out that he tried to _____ me.

4 I'll take you to a fancy restaurant as a birthday _____.

5 It's a _____ to eat *tteokguk* on New Year's Day in Korea.

☀ 생각을 키우는 서술형 • 수행평가 대비 훈련

C 다음 [보기]에서 알맞은 말을 골라 글을 완성하시오.

I had a great time visiting my cousin in America. We _____ Halloween!

First, we shopped for _____ and decorations. I bought a ghost costume, and

my cousin bought green face paint. We also came home with two orange

pumpkins. At home, we _____ out the pumpkins and made them into jack-o'

lanterns. That night, we put them on our _____ and we went out in our

costumes. We got candy and sweet treats. Some adults even played _____

on us. It was a lot of fun!

| 보기 | hollowed | celebrated | tricks | doorstep | costumes |

생각의 폭을 넓히는 **배경지식 Story**

#*Topic* Greenland & Geography

지구에 있는 continent는 모두 몇 개일까요? 정답은 7개입니다. 보통 아시아와 유럽, 아프리카, 북아메리카, 남아메리카, 오세아니아에 매우 추운 남극 대륙까지 더하여 7개의 대륙으로 classify하지요. 그런데 이 대륙들은 맨 처음 지구가 만들어졌을 때도 지금의 모습과 같았을까요?

7개의 대륙이 본래 하나의 땅덩어리였다가 점차 seperate되어 오늘과 같은 모습이 되었다는 scientific 가설을 '대륙 이동설'이라고 해요. 기상학자였던 독일의 베게너는 남아메리카의 동쪽 해안선과 아프리카 대륙의 서쪽 해안선이 잘 맞추어지는 것을 보고 두 대륙이 예전에는 붙어 있었을 것이라는 생각을 하게 되었어요. 그는 대륙들이 geologically 유사할 뿐 아니라, 동떨어진 곳에 위치한 각 area는 자연 환경이 매우 다름에도 불구하고 같은 동식물의 화석이 발견된다는 점, 각 대륙의 산맥들이 지질구조가 비슷하다는 점 등을 근거로 이 대륙들이 오랜 옛날에는 하나의 큰 대륙이었을 것이라는 가설을 세웠죠.

만약 원시 지구에 하나의 대륙만 있었다면, 엄청나게 넓은 바다 위에 떠 있는 거대한 섬처럼 보였겠죠? 생각해보면 우리가 대륙이라고 부르는 큰 땅도 섬처럼 바다로 둘러 쌓여있어요. 그렇다면 섬과 대륙의 status를 나누는 criteria는 무엇일까요? 이어지는 글에서 섬과 대륙, 둘의 차이를 알아보도록 합시다.

본문 미리보기 QUIZ

1   그린란드는 [☐ 국가이다.   ☐ 국가가 아니다.]

66쪽에서 확인

2   섬이 아닌 대륙이 되기 위해서는 [☐ 두 가지   ☐ 네 가지] 기준을 충족해야 한다.

68쪽에서 확인

독해의 장벽을 깨는 만만한 Vocabulary

Study Date: _____ / _____

☐ 1	**attract** [ətrǽkt]	통 끌어들이다	사람들을 끌어들이다	_____ people
☐ 2	**area** [ɛ́əriə]	명 지역, 구역	넓은 지역	a huge _____
☐ 3	**classify** [klǽsəfài]	통 분류하다	책을 분류하다	_____ books
☐ 4	**climate** [kláimit]	명 기후	기후 변화	_____ change
☐ 5	**continent** [kántənənt]	명 대륙	아프리카 대륙	the African _____
☐ 6	**criteria** [kraitíəriə]	명 기준	기준에 맞다	meet the _____
☐ 7	**distinct** [distíŋkt]	형 뚜렷한, 분명한	뚜렷한 특징	a _____ character
☐ 8	**exile** [éɡzail]	통 추방하다 명 망명, 추방	범죄자들을 추방하다	_____ criminals
☐ 9	**geologically** [dʒìːəládʒikəli]	부 지질학상으로	지질학적으로 활발한	_____ active
☐ 10	**local** [lóukəl]	형 지역의, 현지의	현지 시각	_____ time
☐ 11	**murder** [mə́ːrdər]	명 살인(죄)	살인 용의자	a _____ suspect
☐ 12	**scientific** [sàiəntífik]	형 과학적인	과학 지식	_____ knowledge
☐ 13	**separate** [sépərèit]	통 분리하다, 나누다	쓰레기를 분리하다	_____ garbage
☐ 14	**settler** [sétlər]	명 정착민	초기 정착민	an early _____
☐ 15	**status** [stéitəs]	명 신분, 지위	사회적 지위	social _____

어휘 자신만만 QUIZ

1 그린란드라는 이름은 초기 스칸디나비아 정착민들로부터 유래한다.

The name Greenland comes from the early Scandinavian _____.

2 그들은 다른 대륙들과 분리되어 있다.

They are separated from other _____.

Greenland Is Not Very Green

Greenland is the world's largest island. Some people mistakenly think that it is a nation, but it is a self-governing province of Denmark. Greenland lies just south of the Arctic Circle, so it is very cold there. In the winter months, the temperatures are below freezing all day long. In the summer months, highs can go up to 10°C. Contrary to its
5   name, most areas of Greenland are covered with ice.

The name Greenland comes from the early Scandinavian settlers. It is said that Eric the Red, a Norwegian Viking, was exiled from Iceland for murder. Around 980 AD, he and his family moved to Greenland. He named the island Greenland, hoping that the good name would attract other settlers. However, it was only in the 18th century that
10   Danish colonization began.

Greenland is 2.1 million km^2, which means it is ten times as big as the Korean Peninsula. However, Greenland still remains the least densely populated place in the world. Its population is only about 56,000. _____, only 2.7 people live in every 100 km^2. Around 90% of the population is Inuit or mixed Danish and Inuit. The
15   rest are from European origins, mainly Danish. Nearly all Greenlanders live in the southwest of the main island, which has a relatively mild climate. More than 25% of the population lives in the capital, Nuuk.

Words

mistakenly 🔢 잘못하여, 실수로   nation 🔢 국가   self-governing 🔢 자치의   province 🔢 주, 지방
below freezing 영하의   contrary to ~와 반대로   area 🔢 지역, 구역   be covered with ~으로 덮이다
settler 🔢 정착민   exile 🔢 추방하다 🔢 추방, 망명   murder 🔢 살인(죄)   attract 🔢 끌어들이다
colonization 🔢 식민지화   densely populated 인구가 밀집한   mild 🔢 가벼운, 온화한

1 • Title

Match each paragraph with an appropriate title.

(1) Paragraph 1 •　　　　　• a. The Origin of the Name "Greenland"

(2) Paragraph 2 •　　　　　• b. The Size and Population of Greenland

(3) Paragraph 3 •　　　　　• c. The Location and Climate of Greenland

2 • Linking

What is the best choice for the blank?

a. For example　　　　　　b. In other words

c. On the contrary　　　　　d. Unfortunately

3 • Details

Write T if the statement is true and F if it is false.

(1) _____ The temperature in Greenland is always below freezing.

(2) _____ Eric the Red was probably the first to call the island Greenland.

(3) _____ The area of Greenland is far larger than that of Korea.

4 • Graphic Organizer

Complete the map with the words from the passage.

Greenland
Self-governing
province of Denmark

- Size − 2.1 million km^2
- Location − Just _____ of the Arctic Circle
- Climate − Usually temperatures are below _____

- Capital − _____
- Population − about 56,000, mostly Inuit or mixed _____ and Inuit
- Origin of name − named Greenland by _____ the Red

그린란드의 주인, 이누이트

그린란드에 거주하는 주민은 대부분 에스키모인 이누이트와 유럽인의 혼혈이다. 이누이트족은 우리나라와 같은 몽골계 인종으로 유럽인들이 20세기 무렵 그린란드로 본격적으로 이주하기 전부터 이 섬에서 생활해 왔다. 오늘날 활발한 서양 문화의 유입에도 불구하고 이들은 이누이트어 등 자신들만의 독특한 생활양식을 지키기 위해서 노력하고 있다.

▶ 세계에서 가장 큰 섬, 그린란드에 관한 정보를 동영상으로 만나 보세요. ● Time 6' 06''

Continent or Island?

My Reading Time | Words 220 / 2분 26초

1회 ____ 분 ____ 초 2회 ____ 분 ____ 초

Greenland is known as an island while Australia is considered a continent. It appears they should have the same ⓐ status, however, in that they are separated from other continents. What makes the difference?

To be a continent, a piece of land should meet four ⓑ criteria. First, it must be tectonically independent from other continents. Second, it must have biological distinctiveness with unique animal and plant life. Third, it must have unique cultures. Finally, local people must believe it to be a continent. The first two are scientific, whereas the second two are more subjective.

	Australia	Greenland
Tectonic independence	Yes	No
Unique animal and plant life	(A) _____	No
Unique cultures	Yes	No
Local opinion	Continent	(B) _____

The table above shows why Australia is a continent while Greenland is an island. Australia sits on its own tectonic plate whereas Greenland is geologically part of North America. Australia has highly ⓒ distinct plants and animals. In contrast, Greenland's ⓓ wildlife is largely similar to that of North America's. Australia has unique cultures. Greenland's cultures are also unique. Greenland even has its own official language, Greenlandic. However, their cultures can be classified as part of a larger North American culture. Australians often say that Australia is the largest island and the smallest continent as well. People in Greenland, however, say that Greenland is the largest island.

Words

continent 몡 대륙   status 몡 신분, 지위   separate 통 분리하다, 나누다   criteria 몡 기준   tectonically 뿐 지질구조상으로   independent 형 독립된   biological 형 생물학의   unique 형 독특한   local 형 지역의   scientific 형 과학적인   subjective 형 주관적인   geologically 뿐 지질학상으로   distinct 형 뚜렷한, 분명한   wildlife 몡 야생동물   similar 형 비슷한   official 형 공식적인   classify 통 분류하다

Main Idea

1   **What is the main idea of the passage?**

a. Greenland and Australia are both large pieces of land.

b. Greenland and Australia share more similarities than differences.

c. Unlike Greenland, Australia meets the criteria for being a continent.

d. Biological distinctiveness is the most important criteria for being an island.

Inference

2   **What are the best answers for the blanks (A) and (B) in the table?**

(A) → _____   (B) → _____

Words

3   **Which meaning is NOT correct?**

a. ⓐ status: position

b. ⓑ criteria: standards, conditions

c. ⓒ distinct: similar

d. ⓓ wildlife: plants and animals that live in the wild

Summary

4   **Complete the summary using the words from the passage.**

What makes Australia a continent and Greenland an island? There are four _____ for a piece of land to be a continent: _____ from other tectonic plates, _____ animal and plant life, unique _____, and _____ opinion. Australia _____ the criteria, whereas Greenland doesn't.

지식백과

지구 온난화와 그린란드의 얼음

2018년 여름 그린란드 북부 해안의 해빙(sea ice)이 사상 최초로 무너져 내렸다는 CNN 보도가 있었다. 그린란드의 해빙은 두께가 최대 20m가 넘어 북극 얼음의 '마지막 보루'라고 불리던 곳이다. 기후학자들은 북극 지역도 예외가 아닌 기후 변화 현상에 우려를 표했다. 월트 마이어 미 국립설빙데이터센터(NSIDC) 선임 연구원은 "북극 기후가 변하고 있음을 극명하게 보여주는 것"이라고 말했다.

A   Unit 08에서 학습한 단어를 생각해 보고, 다음 퍼즐을 완성해 보시오.

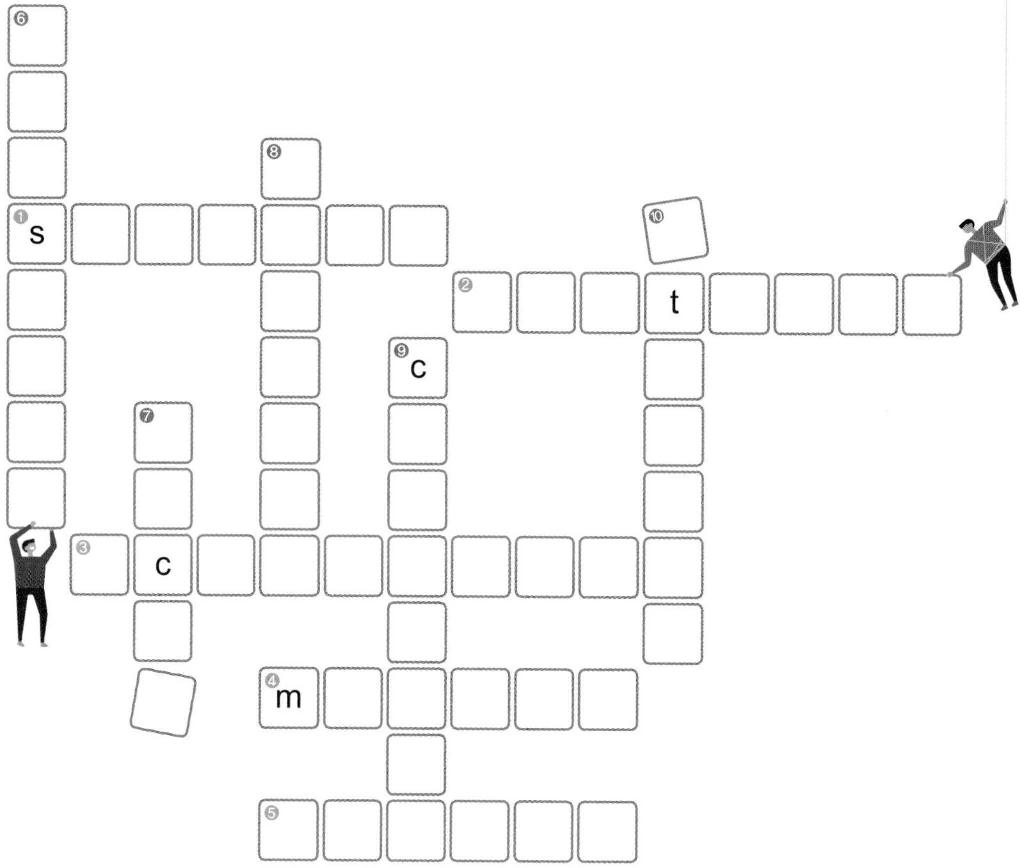

☞ **Across**

❶ someone who moves to a new place where not many people have lived before

❷ clearly different from something else

❸ 과학적 지식: _____ knowledge

❹ the crime of illegally killing of a person

❺ 사회적 지위: social _____

👇 **Down**

❻ _____ the books by subject.
(책들을 주제별로 분류해라.)

❼ 현지 시각: _____ time

❽ the weather conditions in a particular region

❾ the plural form of criterion

❿ to make people interested in something

B 다음 [보기]에서 알맞은 말을 골라 문장을 완성하시오.

> 보기   separate   subjective   exile   attract   continent

1 Asia is the largest _____ in the world.

2 Please _____ food from other wastes.

3 Korea is working hard to _____ tourists from other countries.

4 The king will _____ the criminals to the neighboring country.

5 Knowledge and facts are objective while opinions and beliefs are _____.

🔆 **생각을 키우는 서술형 • 수행평가 대비 훈련**

C 다음 글을 읽고, 밑줄 친 부분 중 어색한 것을 골라 바르게 고치시오.

> Enjoy Greenland, the world's largest island! There are many things to see and do here. To start with, you can experience ⓐnature. Just south of the Arctic Circle, you will see plants and animals in a natural environment. The population is low, so you can go hiking in the ⓑleast densely populated place on Earth. Next, you can experience ⓒculture. Come and see how the Vikings lived, and learn Greenlandic. Or watch a dog race in the snow. Cold? Then go ⓓout of a museum and learn about ⓔearly settlers. Come visit Greenland today!

_____ → _____

생각의 폭을 넓히는 **배경지식 Story**

#*Topic* Gap Year

'갭이어'에 대해 들어본 적이 있나요? '갭이어'란 고등학교까지의 학업을 complete하면 잠시 휴식을 갖고 자신의 흥미나 적성을 찾으며 시간을 spend하는 것을 말해요. 이 기간 동안에는 abroad로 여행을 가거나 자원봉사를 할 수도 있고 평소 배우고 싶었던 기술을 acquire하는 것도 가능하지요. 이렇게 해 보는 opportunity를 갖는 것이 인생에서 essential한 일이라고 생각하는 사람들이 많아지고 있어요.

하버드 대학과 같은 prestigious한 대학들도 갭이어를 장려할 정도로 영어권의 청소년들에게는 갭이어가 익숙하답니다. 우리에게 「해리 포터」 시리즈로 잘 알려진 엠마 왓슨은 이 기간 동안 영화를 촬영했고, 버락 오바마 전 미국 대통령의 딸인 말리아 오바마도 대학에 진학하기에 앞서 갭이어를 보냈다고 해요. 각자 다양한 purpose를 가지고 갭이어를 활용하고 있는 셈이죠.

갭이어는 청소년들이 pursue할 삶의 목표와 가치에 대해 생각해 보도록 motivate를 하는 역할을 해요. 각자의 꿈을 이룰 수 있도록 encourage하는 것이죠. 이어지는 글에서 갭이어에 대해 좀 더 알아봅시다.

본문 미리보기 QUIZ

1   '갭이어'는 젊은이들이 [☐ 대학교를 시작하기 전에 / ☐ 대학교를 마친 후에] 갖는 휴식 시간이다.　**74쪽에서 확인**

2   글쓴이는 아프리카에서 [☐ 지역 아이들을 / ☐ 지역 노인들을] 위한 자원봉사 활동을 했다.　**76쪽에서 확인**

☐ 1	**abroad** [əbrɔ́:d]	閏 해외로	해외를 여행하다	travel _____
☐ 2	**acquire** [əkwáiər]	동 습득하다, 얻다	기술을 습득하다	_____ a skill
☐ 3	**complete** [kəmplí:t]	동 끝마치다	과제를 끝마치다	_____ a task
☐ 4	**dreadful** [drédfəl]	형 끔찍한, 무시무시한	끔찍한 소식	a _____ news
☐ 5	**encourage** [inkə́:ridʒ]	동 격려하다	학생들을 격려하다	_____ students
☐ 6	**equipment** [ikwípmənt]	명 장비, 설비	최첨단 장비	high-tech _____
☐ 7	**essential** [isénʃəl]	형 필수적인	필수적인 요소	an _____ element
☐ 8	**instructional** [instrʌ́kʃənəl]	형 교육용의	교육용 비디오	_____ videos
☐ 9	**momentum** [mouméntəm]	명 가속도	가속도를 얻다	gain _____
☐ 10	**motivate** [móutəvèit]	동 동기를 부여하다	그에게 동기를 부여하다	_____ him
☐ 11	**nearly** [níərli]	閏 거의	거의 빈	_____ empty
☐ 12	**prestigious** [prestídʒəs]	형 명망 있는, 일류의	명문 학교	a _____ school
☐ 13	**purpose** [pə́:rpəs]	명 목적	주된 목적	the prime _____
☐ 14	**pursue** [pərsú:]	동 추구하다	목표를 추구하다	_____ a goal
☐ 15	**spend** [spend]	동 (시간을) 보내다	주말을 보내다	_____ the weekend

어휘 자신만만 QUIZ

1 갭이어에 대한 생각은 1990년대에 가속도가 붙었다.

The idea of a gap year gained _____ in the 1990s.

2 또한 모든 교실에 최첨단 교육 장비가 설치되었다.

High-tech instructional _____ was also installed in every classroom.

Why a Gap Year?

Many young people in English-speaking countries take time off before they start university. This is known as a gap year. A gap year experience can last for several weeks or up to a full year. "Gappers" use this time for different purposes. While some travel or pursue their hobbies, many enjoy doing volunteer work, often abroad.

5　　The concept has its origins in the United Kingdom. In the past, only a small number of students could take a gap year. The idea of a gap year gained momentum in the 1990s. Prince Harry spent a gap year in Africa in 2004. Since then, taking time out has become a rite of passage for tens of thousands of U.K. students. It is becoming popular with U.S. students, too.

10　　Does this time off help the "gappers"? Research says that it does. Students who take a gap year are more focused and motivated when they start to study at college. A gap year gives them the opportunity to learn about the real world and acquire essential life skills. Most importantly, they get a chance to find out about themselves. For these reasons, some of the most prestigious universities are convinced of the benefits of a

15　gap year. Harvard University, _____, encourages every new freshman to consider taking the option seriously.

Words

gap 명 공백, 틈　　take time off 휴가를 내다　　purpose 명 목적　　pursue 동 추구하다　　volunteer work 자원봉사　　abroad 부 해외로　　concept 명 개념　　origin 명 기원　　momentum 명 가속도　　motivate 동 동기를 부여하다　　acquire 동 습득하다, 얻다　　essential 형 필수적인　　encourage 동 격려하다　　prestigious 형 명망있는, 일류의　　be convinced of ~을 확신하다　　benefit 명 혜택, 이득

Topic

1 **Match each paragraph with an appropriate topic.**

(1) Paragraph 1 •   • a. the benefits of a gap year

(2) Paragraph 2 •   • b. the origins and new popularity of the gap year

(3) Paragraph 3 •   • c. the definition of a gap year

Reference

2 **Which is the best choice for the blank?**

a. however   b. for instance

c. in addition   d. in contrast

Details

3 **Which is NOT mentioned as a benefit of taking a gap year?**

a. Students are more focused when they return to school.

b. Students have a chance to make a lot of friends.

c. Students learn some basic life skills.

d. Students find out who they are.

Summary

4 **Complete the summary using the words from the passage.**

> A gap year is when a student takes time off before starting _____. A
> gapper can take one to travel, pursue hobbies, or do _____ work
> abroad. It started in the U.K. Since 2004, it has become _____ in the
> U.K. and in the U.S, too. Taking a gap year helps students _____ on
> their studies better, learn about the real world, and have time to learn about
> _____.

지식백과

덴마크의 에프터스콜레(Efterskole)

영국에 갭이어가 있다면, 덴마크에는 에프터스콜레가 있다. 에프터스콜레는 갭이어와 마찬가지로 초등, 중등 교육을 마치고 고등학교로 진학하기 전 1년간 자신의 진로를 설계하는 프로그램이다. 갭이어와 비교했을 때 에프터스콜레는 일종의 학교 프로그램으로 공교육에 가깝다. 학생들은 이 기간 동안 여러 학생들과 함께 어울려서 토론과 민주적인 의사결정을 통해 학습하고 자신의 진로에 대해 깊이 고민하는 기회를 얻는다.

A Year in Kenya

My Reading Time | Words 228 / 2분 30초

1회 ___분___초   2회 ___분___초

September 23, 2018

It has been nearly a year since I first set foot in Kenya to spend my gap year here. So far, I haven't suffered from any really dreadful diseases that the locals have to deal with. This afternoon, I (A) had / has terrible diarrhea, perhaps because of food poisoning. Thanks to some herbal medicine, however, I feel better now and ready to reflect on what has happened here over the past year.

When I look back, everything in Kenya (B) has been / had been great. The school building project was almost completed. Books and other school supplies arrived, new desks and chairs were brought into the building, and high-tech instructional equipment was also installed in every classroom. The kids from the village will soon study in better classrooms and take breaks on a safer playground. Of course, they will enjoy clean water, too. The new well will give clean water to every kid. I am proud that I could be of help to the kids here.

I didn't know that a gap year in Africa would _____. I realized the importance of teamwork. Also, I learned that helping others makes me happy. I had plenty of opportunities to learn about the local culture and cuisine, too. Tomorrow will be my last day in Kenya, and I will miss everything here, except the horrible diarrhea.

Words

set foot 발을 들여놓다   suffer from ~으로 고생하다   dreadful 휑 끔찍한, 무시무시한   locals 명 현지인들
deal with 다루다, 처리하다   diarrhea 명 설사   reflect on 깊이 생각하다   look back 되돌아보다
school supply 학용품   instructional 휑 교육용의   equipment 명 장비, 용품   install 동 설치하다
plenty of 많은   cuisine 명 요리법, 요리

1 Title

Another title for the passage could be "_____."

a. The Value of Volunteer Work

b. An Exciting Vacation in Africa

c. Feelings About a Gap Year

d. Some Tips for How to Spend a Gap Year

2 Grammar

Choose the words that fit in the boxes (A) and (B).

(A)	(B)		(A)	(B)
a. had	⋯⋯ has been		b. has had	⋯⋯ has been
c. had	⋯⋯ had been		d. has had	⋯⋯ had been

3 Details

Which is the best choice for the blank?

a. pass so quickly

b. be a terrible experience

c. be so boring and dangerous

d. teach me so many valuable lessons

4 Graphic Organizer

Complete the map with the words from the passage.

> **I came to Kenya a year ago to spend my gap year**

What I did	What I learned
• _____ building project • working on classrooms, the playground, and a _____	• the importance of _____ • the happiness of helping others • the local culture and _____

지식백과

많은 사람이 왜 아프리카로 봉사활동을 갈까?

아프리카 대륙은 오랫동안 유럽 국가의 식민지로 수탈당하면서 산업이 발달하지 못했다. 엎친 데 덮친 격으로, 아프리카 대륙의 많은 나라들이 내전과 독재, 극심한 가뭄과 자연재해로 몸살을 겪었고 이는 곧 기본적인 식량과 식수의 부족과 같은 생존의 위협으로까지 이어졌다. 따라서 오늘날 많은 구호단체와 NGO가 이 지역에서 활동하게 되었고, 다양한 사람들의 도움의 손이 이어지고 있다.

▶ 갭이어를 보낸 한국인 학생의 이야기를 동영상으로 감상하세요. ● Time 4' 32''

A   Unit 09에서 학습한 단어를 생각해 보고, 다음 퍼즐을 완성해 보시오.

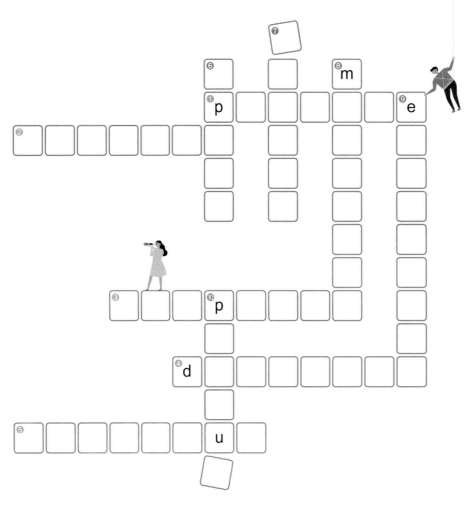

Across

① 의도적으로: on _____

② get knowledge or develop a skill

③ to finish doing something

④ 끔찍한 소식: a _____ news

⑤ 가속도를 얻다: gain _____

Down

⑥ 주말을 보내다: _____ the weekend

⑦ in or to a foreign country

⑧ to make someone have interest in something

⑨ extremely important and necessary

⑩ to try to get or do something over a period of time

B 다음 [보기]에서 알맞은 말을 골라 문장을 완성하시오.

> 보기   encourage   suffer from   cuisine   diarrhea   abroad

1 You can't talk about Korean _____ without kimchi.

2 If you travel _____, you will become more open-minded.

3 The counselor tried to _____ him to express his feelings.

4 If you have had _____ for over two weeks, see your doctor.

5 Because of the construction, the residents _____ dust and noise.

생각을 키우는 서술형 · 수행평가 대비 훈련

C 다음 글을 읽고, 밑줄 친 부분 중 어색한 것을 골라 바르게 고치시오.

> Like my sister, I plan to take a gap year after high school. She went to Kenya, but I don't know where I want to go yet. I just know that I want to ⓐ do volunteer work. Helping others makes me ⓑ happy. But I also want to acquire some valuable life skills. Will ⓒ to help some kids give me that opportunity? I'm not sure. Luckily, my school ⓓ is bringing in a speaker next month. She will tell us about becoming "gappers," explain ⓔ which options are out there, and help us get ready.

_____ → _____

#*Topic* Frida Kahlo, Van Gogh & Self-Portrait

'셀카'는 자신의 얼굴을 자신이 카메라로 직접 찍는 것을 말해요. 요즘 우리는 휴대전화 카메라의 appearance 덕에 어디서나 '셀카'를 찍는 사람들을 볼 수 있어요. '셀카'는 디지털 사회의 self-portrait인 셈이죠. 르네상스 초기부터 수많은 화가들이 자신의 얼굴을 paint한 자화상을 통해 자신을 표현해 왔어요.

자화상을 많이 그린 화가로는 렘브란트가 있어요. 그는 평생 동안 100여 개의 자화상을 그렸다고 하니, amazing하죠? 이런 그의 자화상에는 그의 인생이 depict되어 있어요. 그는 젊은 시절 실력을 인정받아 부와 명성을 얻었지만 이후 사랑하는 아내와 자식을 잃는 pain도 겪어야만 했어요. 그래서 젊은 시절 그의 자화상은 화사하게 그려진 반면, 나이가 든 후의 자화상은 고통을 suffer하는 노인의 모습이 reveal되어 있어요. 그래서 화가의 자화상은 자신을 반영하는 mirror이자 그의 내면세계에 대한 exploration이라고 말할 수 있나봐요.

렘브란트 뿐 아니라 많은 화가들이 자신의 자화상을 그렸어요. 혹시 프리다 칼로를 알고 있나요? 멕시코의 화가인 그녀 역시 자화상으로 well-known하죠. 이어지는 글에서는 프리다 칼로와 자화상에 대해 설명하고 있답니다. 함께 읽어볼까요?

본문 미리보기 QUIZ

1   프리다 칼로의 작품에서 공통적인 주제는 [☐ 행복 ☐ 고통] 이다.   82쪽에서 확인

2   자화상이 본격적으로 유행하게 된 것은 [☐ 15세기 ☐ 19세기] 였다.   84쪽에서 확인

☐ 1	**amazing** [əméiziŋ]	형 놀라운	놀라운 이야기들	_____ stories
☐ 2	**appearance** [əpíərəns]	명 출현, 등장	갑작스러운 출현	sudden _____
☐ 3	**crippled** [krípld]	형 다리를 저는	다리를 저는 남자	a _____ man
☐ 4	**depict** [dipíkt]	동 그리다, 묘사하다	경치를 묘사하다	_____ a scene
☐ 5	**elsewhere** [elswɛər]	부 다른 곳에	딴 곳을 보다	look _____
☐ 6	**exploration** [èkspləréiʃən]	명 탐험, 연구	우주 탐험	space _____
☐ 7	**mentally** [méntəli]	부 정신적으로	정신적으로 피로한	_____ tired
☐ 8	**mirror** [mírər]	명 거울	거울을 보다	look in a _____
☐ 9	**pain** [pein]	명 고통, 통증	예리한 통증	a sharp _____
☐ 10	**reveal** [rivíːl]	동 드러내다	비밀을 드러내다	_____ a secret
☐ 11	**self-portrait** [sélf-pɔ́ːrtrit]	명 자화상	자화상을 그리다	paint a _____
☐ 12	**strength** [streŋθ]	명 힘, 용기	신체적인 힘	physical _____
☐ 13	**suffer** [sʌ́fər]	동 고통받다	~으로 고통받다	_____ from
☐ 14	**therapy** [θérəpi]	명 치료	언어 치료	speech _____
☐ 15	**well-known** [wél-nóun]	형 유명한, 잘 알려진	유명한 소설가	a _____ novelist

어휘 자신만만 QUIZ

1 그녀는 정말로 놀라운 강인함을 지닌 여성이다.

She is indeed a woman of _____ strength.

2 그의 자화상은 거울에 나타나는 대로 얼굴을 묘사한다.

His self-portraits _____ the face as it appeared in the mirror.

"I am not sick. I am broken. But I am happy as long as I can paint."

Can you guess who said this? It was Frida Kahlo. She is a well-known Mexican painter (A) who / whose works of art are highly regarded around the world. She was an amazing woman. Although her life was filled with physical and emotional pain, she never allowed it to take control of her.

Frida Kahlo was born in 1907 in Coyoacan, Mexico. At six, she suffered from polio. At 18, she was injured in a car accident, and her body was almost destroyed. Her doctor didn't expect her to survive. She had to have 35 operations and was never able to have a baby. It was during her stay in hospital (B) that / where Frida Kahlo began to paint.

Frida Kahlo produced 143 paintings. Fifty-five of the paintings are self-portraits. Her

works show the events in her life, her emotions, and the changes in her feelings. Pain is a common theme in her works, which are often violent-looking and bloody. However, Frida Kahlo's paintings simply show what was happening to her. Her paintings are the most honest expressions of herself. Despite all the pain in her life, she continued to paint. She was indeed a woman of amazing strength.

Words well-known 형 유명한, 잘 알려진   highly 부 대단히, 매우   regard 동 ~을 평가하다   physical 형 신체적인   emotional 형 감정적인   pain 명 고통   control 명 지배, 통제   suffer from ~으로 고통 받다   injure 동 부상을 입히다   destroy 동 파괴하다   self-portrait 명 자화상   strength 명 힘, 용기

1 • Title

Another title for the passage could be "_____."

a. Frida Kahlo's Early Life

b. Frida Kahlo, an Incredible Painter

c. Different Expressions of Self Through Art

d. The Amazing Physical Strength of an Artist

2 • Details

Write T if the statement about Frida Kahlo is true and F if it is false.

(1) _____ She is a famous artist who suffered physically and emotionally.

(2) _____ Her baby was seriously injured and endured many operations.

(3) _____ She expressed herself through her works of art.

3 • Grammar

Choose the words that fit in boxes (A) and (B).

	(A)	(B)		(A)	(B)
a.	who	⋯⋯ where	b.	whose	⋯⋯ where
c.	whose	⋯⋯ that	d.	who	⋯⋯ that

4 • Summary

Complete the summary with the words from the passage.

Frida Kahlo is a famous Mexican _____ who endured much pain. She had _____ at 6 and was seriously injured in a car accident at 18. She began to paint while in the _____. Many of her paintings are _____ in which she honestly shows herself. She was an amazing woman who continued to _____ in spite of all her difficulties.

지식백과

내 마음속의 디에고

프리다 칼로가 평생 동안 사랑했던 남편인 디에고 리베라는 그녀에게 사랑과 고통을 동시에 안겨준 대상이었다. 디에고 리베라는 멕시코의 유명한 화가였는데 프리다는 그를 예술과 이념을 공유하는 동지로 생각했다. <내 마음속의 디에고>라는 작품에는 이런 디에고에 대한 프리다 칼로의 사랑이 잘 나타나있는데, 멕시코 전통의상을 입고 있는 그녀의 이마에 디에고 얼굴이 그려져 있다.

The Art of Painting Oneself

🕐 My Reading Time │ Words 211 / 2분 20초

1회 ____분 ____초   2회 ____분 ____초

Self-portraits are pictures artists paint of themselves. Self-portraits have been made since the earliest times. However, it only became a serious trend in the 15th century. With the appearance of better and cheaper mirrors, artists could easily model for their own works of art.

One of the most famous self-portrait artists was Vincent van Gogh. He completed 37 self-portraits between 1886 and 1889. (A) He may have painted so many self-portraits because he didn't have enough money to pay for a professional model. (B) He usually looks elsewhere. (C) His self-portraits depict his face as it appeared in the mirror. (D) So, his right side in the picture is in reality the left side of his face.

The story of Frida Kahlo, another artist known for painting herself, can be read in her self-portraits. About one-third of her work is the exploration of herself, physically and mentally. Kahlo created 55 self-portraits as a kind of therapy to face the most troubling events in her life. In reality, she wore a long dress and covered herself with jewelry to hide her crippled leg and broken body. In her self-portraits, however, she comes out from hiding and reveals her pain. She lets out her feelings on her canvases.

:·: **Words**   trend 몡 유행, 경향   appearance 몡 출현   professional 혱 전문적인   elsewhere 뷔 다른 곳에서

   depict 통 그리다, 묘사하다   exploration 몡 탐험, 연구   mentally 뷔 정신적으로   therapy 몡 치료

reality 몡 현실   jewelry 몡 보석   crippled 혱 불구의, 다리를 저는   reveal 통 드러내다

Topic

1 The first paragraph is mainly about _____.

a. the art of the 15th century

b. the development of mirrors

c. the life of professional models

d. the development of self-portraits

Organization

2 Where would the following sentence best fit?

In his self-portraits, he seldom looks directly at us.

a. (A)   b. (B)   c. (C)   d. (D)

Details

3 Fill in each blank with one word from the passage.

(1) Vincent van Gogh may have been too poor to pay for _____ models.

(2) Frida Kahlo painted self-portraits as a type of _____.

Graphic Organizer

4 Complete the map with the words from the passage.

The World of Self-Portraits		
Development	became popular because of cheaper mirrors in the 15th century	
Famous artists	Vincent van Gogh	• finished _____ self-portraits between 1886 and 1889 • painted self-portraits since he didn't have enough _____ • seldom looks _____ at us in his self-portraits
	Frida Kahlo	• created 55 self-portraits • showed herself physically and _____ • faced the troubling events in her life in her self-portraits

고통을 예술로 승화시킨 작가들

프리다 칼로는 사고 후유증 때문에 겪은 신체적 고통과 남편 디에고로 인한 심적 고통을 자신의 자화상으로 표현했고, 고흐 또한 자신의 정신적 고통을 특유의 화풍에 담아냈다. 프리다 칼로나 고흐처럼 많은 화가들이 자신의 고통을 예술로 승화시켰는데, 프란시스 고야도 그러한 예술가 중 하나이다. 고야와 그의 아내는 무려 6번의 아이를 잃고 7번째에야 첫 아들을 얻을 수 있었다. 고야는 아이를 잃은 자신의 말할 수 없는 고통을 후일 <아들을 잡아먹는 사투르누스>라는 그림으로 표현했다.

▶ 조선 후기의 선비 화가 윤두서의 자화상을 동영상으로 감상해 보세요. ⏱ Time 2' 59''

A Unit 10에서 학습한 단어를 생각해 보고, 다음 퍼즐을 완성해 보시오.

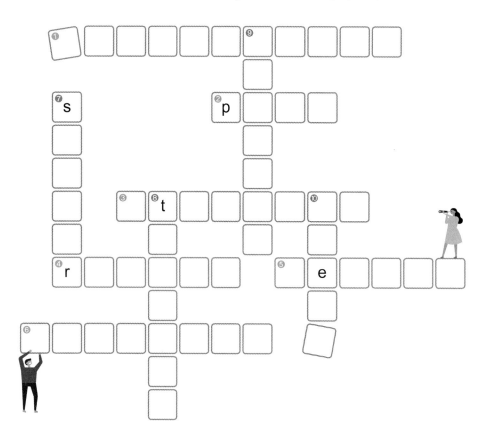

Across

❶ 우주 탐험: space _____

❷ the feelings that you have in your body caused by injury or illness

❸ 신체적인 힘: physical _____

❹ to make known something that was previously unknown

❺ to show someone or something in a picture

❻ 정신적으로 피로한: _____ tired

Down

❼ to be affected by something bad or unpleasant

❽ the treatment of an illness or injury

❾ 놀라운 이야기: an _____ story

❿ a general direction in which something is developing

B 다음 [보기]에서 알맞은 말을 골라 문장을 완성하시오.

보기   depict   reveal   destroy   injure   well-known

1 The man wearing a mask is a _____ actor.

2 Her paintings _____ scenes from everyday life.

3 He didn't want to _____ his secret, but he had to.

4 It is possible that you could _____ yourself during P.E. class.

5 If people continue to _____ the rainforest, our planet will be in danger soon.

생각을 키우는 서술형·수행평가 대비 훈련

C 다음 [보기]에서 알맞은 말을 골라 글을 완성하시오.

Many women artists produce self-portraits. Almost all highly _____ women painters have done at least one. This may be due to culture. Until the 20th century, most women artists weren't able to train with _____ models. So many became portrait painters. In their _____, the most common theme is work. The artist often portrays _____ working, with a brush in one hand. However, often, the beautiful dress in the portrait doesn't look like work clothes. Is it the artist's real dress or an example of _____ expression?

보기   artistic   regarded   self-portraits   professional   herself

생각의 폭을 넓히는 배경지식 Story

#*Topic* Pluto, Eris & Trojan War

에리스(Eris)는 그리스 mythology에 등장하는 discord의 goddess이며, 사람들 사이에 다툼과 분쟁을 일으킨다고 해요. 에리스는 올림푸스산에서 열린 결혼식에 유일하게 초대받지 못한 것을 알았어요. Outraged한 에리스는 황금의 사과에 "가장 아름다운 이에게(To the fairest)"라는 문구를 적어 던졌어요. 이것을 본 헤라, 아테네, 그리고 아프로디테의 세 goddess 사이에 큰 debate가 일어났어요. 서로 황금 사과 ownership을 claim하고 나선 것이죠. 이 골치 아픈 싸움은 결국 그리스의 legendary한 전쟁, 트로이 전쟁의 발단이 되었답니다.

불화의 여신 에리스를 달가워하지 않는 것은 누구나 마찬가지일 거예요. 하지만 에리스에게는 두 가지 모습이 있어서, 한편으로는 불화를 일으키지만 다른 한편으로는 인간의 경쟁심을 부추겨서 자신의 능력을 develop하게 하는 유익한 점도 있다고 해요. 그래도 여전히 그녀의 이름은 우리에게 discord를 떠올리게 해요.

우리 은하에는 2006년에 공식적으로 Eris라고 이름 붙여진 천체가 있어요. 어째서 이런 이름을 붙이게 되었는지 그 이유를 짐작할 수 있나요? 본문에서 함께 확인해 봅시다.

본문 미리보기 QUIZ

1 Pluto와 Eris는 [☐ 행성 / ☐ 왜행성]으로 분류된다. 90쪽에서 확인

2 트로이 전쟁은 트로이의 [☐ 승리 / ☐ 패배]로 끝났다. 92쪽에서 확인

☐ 1	**belong** [bilɔ́ːŋ]	통 ~에 속하다	한국에 속하다	_____ to Korea
☐ 2	**claim** [kleim]	통 주장하다	강하게 주장하다	strongly _____
☐ 3	**debate** [dibéit]	명 논쟁, 토론	열띤 논쟁	a heated _____
☐ 4	**deceive** [disíːv]	통 속이다	서로를 속이다	_____ each other
☐ 5	**develop** [divéləp]	통 발달하다, 발달시키다	기술을 발전시키다	_____ the technology
☐ 6	**discord** [dískɔːrd]	명 불화, 다툼	심각한 불화	serious _____
☐ 7	**dominant** [dámənənt]	형 지배적인	지배적인 위치	a _____ position
☐ 8	**dwarf** [dwɔːrf]	형 왜소한	왜행성, 왜소행성	a _____ planet
☐ 9	**goddess** [gádis]	명 여신	사랑의 여신	the _____ of love
☐ 10	**legendary** [léʤəndèri]	형 전설적인	전설적인 인물	a _____ figure
☐ 11	**mythology** [miθálədʒi]	명 신화	그리스 신화	Greek _____
☐ 12	**outraged** [áutreidʒd]	형 격분한	격분한 시민들	_____ citizens
☐ 13	**ownership** [óunərʃip]	명 소유, 소유권	소유권을 얻다	get _____
☐ 14	**propose** [prəpóuz]	통 제안하다	계획을 제안하다	_____ a plan
☐ 15	**stable** [stéibl]	형 안정적인	안정적인 조건	a _____ condition

어휘 자신만만 QUIZ

1 명왕성이 행성인지 아닌지에 대해 오랜 논쟁이 있어 왔다.

There had been a long _____ about whether Pluto was a planet or not.

2 나머지 그리스 사람들은 트로이 사람들을 속이기 위해 배를 타고 떠났다.

The rest of the Greeks sailed away to _____ the Trojans.

Pluto and Eris

● My Reading Time ㅣ Words 239 / 2분 38초

1회 _____ 분 _____ 초   2회 _____ 분 _____ 초

At the meeting of the IAU (International Astronomical Union) in August 2006, Pluto lost its status as a planet. From its discovery in 1930 until 2006, Pluto was considered the solar system's ninth planet. Under the new IAU definition of a planet, however, Pluto no longer meets the criteria and was reclassified as a dwarf planet.

5

> **The New Definition of a Planet**
>
> A planet is any object in orbit around the Sun
> – with a diameter greater than 2,000 km,
> – whose shape is stable due to its own gravity,
> – that is dominant in its immediate neighborhood.

10 Pluto was much smaller than the other eight planets. So there had been a long debate about whether Pluto was a planet or not. The debate had intensified after the discovery of a massive object, called 2003 UB313, in 2005. ⓐ It is approximately 2,300 kilometers in diameter and a little larger than ⓑ Pluto. At first, it was discussed whether the newly-discovered object would be the tenth planet. At the 2006 IAU

15 meeting, however, ⓒ it was also classified as a dwarf planet, along with Pluto. They were not dominant in their neighborhood.

ⓓ The object was officially named Eris on September 13, 2006. The name was proposed by the discovery team. Eris is the Greek goddess whose greatest joy is to make trouble. The name Eris is a perfect fit for the object considering it brought about

20 one of the largest debates in the astronomical community.

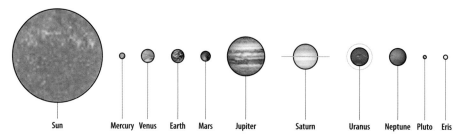

Sun   Mercury Venus   Earth   Mars   Jupiter   Saturn   Uranus Neptune Pluto Eris

Words

Pluto 명 명왕성   status 명 지위   definition 명 정의   meet 동 충족시키다   criteria 명 기준
reclassify 동 재분류하다   dwarf planet 왜행성   orbit 명 궤도   stable 형 안정적인   gravity 명 중력
dominant 형 지배적인   immediate 형 바로 이웃의, 인접한   intensify 동 격렬해지다   massive 형 거
대한   approximately 부 약, 대략   astronomical community 천문학계

1
● Title

Another title for the passage could be "_____."

a. How Pluto Got Its Name

b. Three Criteria for Being a Planet

c. Why Pluto Is No Longer a Planet

d. Eris, Planet or Dwarf Planet?

2
● Reference

Among ⓐ~ⓓ, which refers to something different?

a. ⓐ　　　　b. ⓑ　　　　c. ⓒ　　　　d. ⓓ

3
● Details

Why can't Pluto be a planet?

a. It is not in orbit around the Sun.

b. Its diameter is not greater than 2,000 km.

c. Its shape is not stable.

d. It is not dominant in its immediate neighborhood.

4
● Summary

Complete the summary using the words from the passage.

Pluto was no longer considered a _____ after the IAU meeting in 2006. The discovery of 2003 UB313, which is a little bigger than Pluto, caused an intense _____ about what should be called a planet. Under the new _____ of a planet, both were classified as "dwarf planets" since they were not _____ in their neighborhood. 2003 UB313 was named _____ after the Greek goddess of discord.

지식백과

소행성 이야기

소행성은 태양 주위를 도는 천체 중 행성보다 작은 것을 말한다. 이 중 가장 먼저 발견된 것은 세레스로, 1801년에 발견되었다. 발견된 소행성은 발견자가 이름을 붙일 수 있는데, 처음에는 세레스처럼 주로 그리스·로마 신화의 신들의 이름을 붙였다. 그러나 더 이상 마땅한 이름이 없자 배우자와 아이들의 이름을 붙이거나 도시 이름, 심지어는 애완견의 이름을 붙이는 등 여러 가지 특이한 이름들이 등장하기 시작했다.

The Trojan War

The Trojan War is the greatest war in Greek mythology. It developed from the wedding of Peleus and Thetis. All the gods were invited to their wedding except Eris, the goddess of discord. The angry goddess turned up anyway and threw a golden apple onto the table. She said the apple belonged to the fairest. Hera,
5   Athena and Aphrodite all claimed ownership of the apple.

Zeus proclaimed that Paris, prince of Troy, would act as the judge. Hera promised him power, Athena promised him wisdom and skill in war, and Aphrodite promised him _____. Paris chose Aphrodite. Aphrodite told Paris that Helen, wife of Menelaus, would be his wife. Paris left for Sparta and took
10 Helen to Troy. Menelaus was outraged and asked other Greek kings (A) <u>join</u> the war against Troy. That's how the legendary war started.

Nine years after the war (B) <u>break</u> out, the Greeks still couldn't break down the walls of Troy. Odysseus ordered Greek soldiers to build a large wooden horse which was hollow. Once the statue was built, Odysseus and some soldiers hid
15 inside of it. The rest of the Greeks sailed away to deceive the Trojans. The Trojans thought the Greeks had left and celebrated their victory. They brought the wooden horse as a trophy into the city. That night, after most of Troy had fallen asleep, the Greek soldiers came down from the horse and attacked. The plan
20 brought an end to the war.

Words

mythology 뗑 신화   develop 뙝 발달하다, 발달시키다   except 뗀 ~을 제외하고   discord 뗑 불화, 다툼
belong to ~에게 속하다   claim 뙝 주장하다   ownership 뗑 소유   proclaim 뙝 선언하다   wisdom 뗑
지혜   outraged 뚱 격분한   legendary 뚱 전설적인   hollow 뚱 (속이) 빈   sail 뙝 항해하다   deceive
뙝 속이다   celebrate 뙝 축하하다   trophy 뗑 전리품

Topic

1 This passage is mainly about _____.

a. who made a plan to end the Trojan War

b. how the Trojan War started and ended

c. how Paris' choice influenced the Trojan War

d. how Eris, the goddess of discord got her name

Inference

2 Which is the best choice for the blank?

a. wisdom   b. the biggest country

c. strength   d. the most beautiful woman

Grammar

3 What are the correct forms of the underlined (A) and (B)?

(A) → _____   (B) → _____

Graphic Organizer

4 Complete the chart with the words from the passage.

Cause		Effect
Eris was not invited to a wedding. She got angry, and brought a (1)_____ apple.	→	Three goddesses argued for the (2)_____ of the apple.
Paris chose (3)_____. He took Helen, (4)_____ of Menelaus to Troy.	→	Menelaus asked other Greek kings to join in the war against Troy.
The Greeks built a large (5)_____ (6)_____ and hid inside it.	→	The soldiers destroyed Troy, bringing an end to the war.

그리스 신화의 파리스(Paris) 이야기

지식 백과

파리스는 트로이의 왕자로 태어났으나, 그가 트로이를 망하게 할 것이라는 이유로 버려졌던 인물이다. 요정 오이노네와 이미 행복하게 살고 있었던 그는 황금 사과의 주인을 가려달라는 판결을 맡게 되는데, 결국 권력이나 전쟁에서의 승리 대신에 가장 아름다운 여성을 선택하는 어리석은 행동을 하게 된다. 당시 세계에서 가장 아름다운 여성은 스파르타의 왕 메넬라우스의 아내 헬렌이었다. 따라서 파리스는 아프로디테가 약속한 헬렌을 데려왔고 이로 인해 트로이 전쟁이 시작되었다. 전쟁 중에 그는 독화살을 맞고 쓰러졌으나 치료약이 있던 오이노네의 외면으로 죽고 만다.

▶ 파리스에 대해 동영상으로 좀 더 알아 보세요. ● Time 7' 47''

Reading Closer

독해의 내공을 키우는 마무리 학습

A

Unit 11에서 학습한 단어를 생각해 보고, 다음 퍼즐을 완성해 보시오.

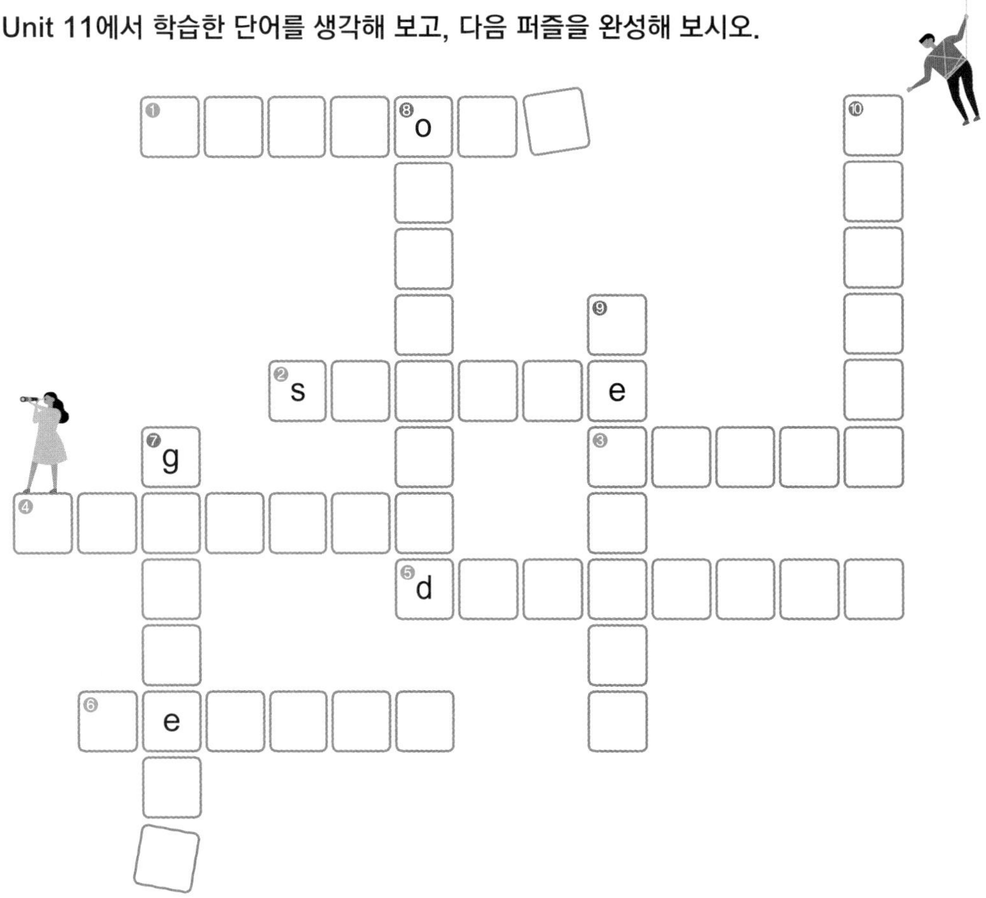

Across

❶ disagreement between people

❷ not likely to suddenly change

❸ 강하게 주장하다: strongly ________

❹ to suggest a possible plan or idea to consider

❺ more important or strong than the other things

❻ a discussion about a subject in which people have different opinions

Down

❼ 사랑의 여신: ________ of love

❽ 격분한 시민들: ________ citizens

❾ to make someone believe something that is not true

❿ 전쟁에서의 지혜와 기술: ________ and skill in war

B 다음 [보기]에서 알맞은 말을 골라 문장을 완성하시오.

> 보기   dominant   stable   proclaim   belong   approximately

1 Napoleon went on to _____ himself emperor.

2 She spent _____ eight hours struggling with the problem.

3 Because he was always alone, he thought he didn't _____ there.

4 The company holds a _____ position in the mobile device market.

5 Thanks to the smooth supply of raw materials, the market remained _____.

🔆 **생각을 키우는 서술형·수행평가 대비 훈련**

C 다음 글을 읽고, 밑줄 친 부분 중 어색한 것을 골라 바르게 고치시오.

Pluto the planet or *Pluto the dog*: which name came first? They both became ⓐ <u>dominant</u> in modern culture in about 1931. The planet Pluto was considered the solar system's ninth ⓑ <u>planet</u>. Meanwhile, the dog named Pluto was also part of a group. He was one of the six biggest stars in the Disney universe. But ⓒ <u>which</u> came first? An 11-year-old British girl ⓓ <u>suggested</u> the name for the planet. She said that she did ***not*** name it after Disney's dog. ⓔ <u>Therefore</u>, the debate continues because Disney has never explained the legendary dog's name.

_____ → _____

#Topic Whale & Environment

바다에서 가장 큰 동물인 whale을 본 적 있나요? 이 동물의 majestic한 외형을 보면 누구나 할 말을 잃게 될 거예요. 고래는 서로 의사소통을 하며 사냥을 할 정도로 매우 intelligent한 동물이라고 해요. 그런데 고래는 marine의 동물이긴 하지만, 어류로 분류되지는 않아요. 이유가 무엇일까요?

먼저 고래는 다른 물고기처럼 아가미로 숨을 쉬지 않고, 바다의 surface로 올라와서 허파로 숨을 쉬어요. 한 번 수면 위로 float한 고래는 가능한 한 많은 공기를 들이마시는데, 고래의 피에는 헤모글로빈이 많아서 오랫동안 물속에 sink한 채로 있을 수 있답니다. 결정적으로, 고래는 알을 낳는 것이 아니라 새끼를 낳아서 젖을 먹여 키워요. 이런 biological한 특징들을 바탕으로 고래를 포유류로 분류하죠. 참 흥미로운 동물이죠?

하지만 고래는 사람들의 frequent한 포획 때문에 멸종 위기에 처하는 tragedy를 겪었어요. 이렇게 giant하고 intelligent한 동물도 인간의 무자비한 사냥 앞에서는 속수무책이었던 거예요. 고래를 지키기 위해서 우리 모두의 관심이 필요해요! 이어지는 글에서 고래에 대해 좀 더 알아볼까요?

sperm whale(향유고래)

본문 미리보기 QUIZ

1 고래가 해변에 누운 채로 [☐ 해수욕을 하는 / ☐ 죽어가고 있는] 모습이 발견되곤 한다. 98쪽에서 확인

2 고래의 [☐ 하품 / ☐ 배설물] 은 환경에 좋은 영향을 끼치고 있다. 100쪽에서 확인

☐ 1	**abandon** [əbǽndən]	통 버리다	희망을 버리다	_____ hope
☐ 2	**biological** [bàiəlάdʒikəl]	형 생물학적인	생물학적 기능들	_____ functions
☐ 3	**disrupt** [disrʌ́pt]	통 방해하다	회의를 방해하다	_____ the meeting
☐ 4	**float** [flout]	통 떠다니다	자유롭게 떠다니다	freely _____
☐ 5	**frequent** [frí:kwənt]	형 잦은, 빈번한	빈번한 방문	_____ visits
☐ 6	**giant** [dʒáiənt]	형 거대한	거대한 고릴라	a _____ gorilla
☐ 7	**intelligent** [intélədʒənt]	형 총명한, 똑똑한	총명한 아이들	_____ children
☐ 8	**majestic** [mədʒéstik]	형 장엄한	장엄한 경관	_____ scenery
☐ 9	**marine** [mərí:n]	형 바다의, 해양의	해양 동물	a _____ animal
☐ 10	**sink** [siŋk]	통 가라앉다	바닥으로 가라앉다	_____ to the bottom
☐ 11	**shallow** [ʃǽlou]	형 얕은	얕은 물	_____ water
☐ 12	**surface** [sə́:rfis]	명 표면, 지면	빛나는 표면	a shiny _____
☐ 13	**tragedy** [trǽdʒədi]	명 비극	끔찍한 비극	a terrible _____
☐ 14	**undertake** [ʌ̀ndərtéik]	통 착수하다	과제에 착수하다	_____ the task
☐ 15	**whale** [weil]	명 고래	고래의 개체 수	_____ population

어휘 자신만만 QUIZ

1 그것은 비극인데 우리는 왜 그런 일이 생기는지 알지 못한다.

It is a _____, and we don't know why it happens.

2 우리는 도시에서 나오는 생물학적 쓰레기를 제거하기 위한 프로젝트를 수행한다.

We undertake projects to get rid of _____ waste from cities.

Whales on the Beach

🕐 My Reading Time | Words 227 / 2분 30초

1회 ____ 분 ____ 초   2회 ____ 분 ____ 초

In February 2011, a pod of 107 whales was found beached on Stewart Island, New Zealand. A few weeks earlier, on the coast of South Island in New Zealand, a pod of 80 pilot whales had been found. Today there are still frequent reports of whales lying helpless and dying on the beach. How do some of the most intelligent animals get
5 stranded on the beach in many parts of the world? It is a tragedy, and we don't know why it happens. Scientists are still searching for clues that will unlock this mystery.

There are some theories about why whales swim into shallow water and get stranded. First, the pod follows a sick whale on shore to help it, and becomes stuck. As whales are very social, the other healthy whales refuse to abandon their sick friend.

10 Another theory is related to navy*sonar, which is a measuring technique using sound and echoes. Some scientists say that the low-frequency and mid-frequency sonar used by navies can disrupt an animal's navigation system, causing it to lose its way, stray into shallow water, and end up trapped on the beach.

Besides the above two most common theories, there are other possible causes,
15 which include weather conditions, magnetic field anomalies, diseases, etc. Whatever the cause may be, it won't be easy to stop the mass strandings of these majestic creatures.

* **sonar** 수중 음파 탐지기

Words pod 명 (고래 등의) 작은 떼　beached 형 해변으로 쓸려 온　frequent 형 잦은, 빈번한　helpless 형 무기력한　intelligent 형 총명한, 똑똑한　strand 동 좌초시키다　tragedy 명 비극　shallow 형 얕은　shore 명 해안, 물가　refuse 동 거부하다　abandon 동 버리다　navy 명 해군　disrupt 동 방해하다　theory 명 이론　magnetic field anomaly 자기장 이상　majestic 형 장엄한

Title

1 Another title for the passage could be "_____."

a. The Intelligence about Whales

b. Some Theories about Whale Strandings

c. How to Avoid Being Trapped on the Beach

d. Dangers to a Pod of Whales in Shallow Water

Words

2 What does the underlined abandon mean?

a. follow   b. catch

c. disrupt   d. desert

Details

3 Navy sonar can _____.

a. cause a stomachache in whales

b. be used to guide whales in shallow water

c. cause whales to lose their sense of direction

d. be used to change whales' social behavior

Graphic Organizer

4 Complete the map with the words from the passage.

Mass Strandings of Whales

Problem	Whales get _____ on the beach in many parts of the world.

↓

Theory 1	The pod follows a _____ whale on shore, and becomes stuck in the _____ water.
Theory 2	Navy sonar disrupts a whale's _____ system and causes it to _____ its way.
Other theories	Weather conditions, _____ _____ anomalies, diseases, etc.

지식 백과

향유고래와 「모비 딕」

향유고래는 몸길이 10~20m, 몸무게가 약 40~50톤에 이르는 거대한 생물이다. 예로부터 사람들은 향유고래를 잡아 용연향이라는 값비싼 향료를 얻거나 머리에서 기름을 얻었다. 허만 멜빌의 유명한 소설인 「모비 딕」의 주인공이 바로 이 향유고래인데, 선장인 아합(Ahab)이 하얀 고래 모비 딕을 잡기 위해 분투하는 것이 소설의 주요 내용이다. 「모비 딕」에는 고래에 대한 섬세한 묘사와 더불어 고래의 기름을 채취하는 방법이나 고래잡이 선원들의 생활상이 매우 자세하게 그려져 있다.

Here on land, we undertake great engineering projects to get rid of biological waste from cities and livestock farms. What about the sea, where huge animals produce a lot of waste? A recent study suggests that sperm whales in the Southern Ocean have the ability to offset greenhouse gases with their poop. Whale poop

5   pulls carbon dioxide from the atmosphere and moves it to the bottom of the ocean.

How does it work? Sperm whales dive deep in the ocean, (A) which / where they feed on squid. They come back to the surface to breathe and, while they are at it, they poop a floating stream of liquid. The whale poop showers over minute

10   plants floating on the surface. Because it is rich in iron, their poop helps stimulate plankton growth in the ocean. The plankton take in carbon dioxide from the atmosphere and eventually sink to the bottom of the ocean.

These ocean giants and certain other marine mammals may, therefore, be among the most environmentally friendly animals on the planet. Australian

15   biologists estimated that about 12,000 sperm whales live in the Southern Ocean. According to the researchers, one sperm whale can take care of roughly 200,000 tons of carbon dioxide a year. This is equal to the amount of carbon dioxide (B) given / giving off by 40,000 cars. Unfortunately, however, the whale population is decreasing. If whale poop indeed cleans the environment, shouldn't

20   we make sure that whales are protected?

Words poop 몡 배설물   undertake 통 착수하다   biological 혱 생물학적인   livestock 몡 가축   sperm whale 향유고래   offset 통 상쇄하다   atmosphere 몡 대기   squid 몡 오징어   minute 혱 극미한, 극히 작은   stimulate 통 자극하다, 활발하게 하다   eventually 뿐 결국   marine 혱 바다의, 해양의   mammal 몡 포유동물   estimate 통 추산하다   roughly 뿐 대략, 약

Main Idea

1 What is the main idea of the passage?

a. Whales are in danger of extinction.

b. Whales should be protected and studied more.

c. Whales clean the bottom of the ocean with their poop.

d. Whales can reduce greenhouse gases with their poop.

Inference

2 Which one is true according to the passage?

a. Whales usually poop at the bottom of the ocean.

b. Sperm whales feed on plankton and minute plants.

c. Marine waste from huge animals like whales causes serious problems.

d. One sperm whale can take care of carbon dioxide from about 40,000 cars.

Grammar

3 Choose the words that fit in boxes (A) and (B).

	(A)		(B)			(A)		(B)
a.	which	⋯⋯	given		b.	where	⋯⋯	given
c.	which	⋯⋯	giving		d.	where	⋯⋯	giving

Summary

4 Complete the summary using the words from the passage.

Whale _____ cleans the environment. They poop at the _____ of the ocean. The poop is rich in _____ and helps _____ grow. Plankton take in _____ _____ from the atmosphere and sink to the ocean floor. One sperm whale can take care of about 200,000 tons of carbon dioxide a year. Unfortunately, however, the whale population is _____.

지식 백과

그리스 신화 속 돌고래

인간에게 매우 친밀한 돌고래는 그리스 신화에도 등장한다. 바다의 신 포세이돈은 바다의 여왕인 암피트라테에게 청혼하지만 그녀는 이를 거절하고 깊은 바다 속에 숨는다. 암피트라테를 너무나 사랑했던 포세이돈은 돌고래에게 그녀를 찾아 줄 것을 부탁한다. 돌고래는 전 세계를 돌아다닌 끝에 바다의 여왕을 찾아 포세이돈의 사랑을 전달해 준다. 후에 포세이돈은 돌고래를 하늘의 별로 만들어 주었다고 한다.

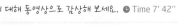 고래에 대해 동영상으로 감상해 보세요. ⏱ Time 7' 42''

Reading Closer

독해의 내공을 키우는 **마무리 학습**

A Unit 12에서 학습한 단어를 생각해 보고, 다음 퍼즐을 완성해 보시오.

👉 **Across**

❶ to go down below the surface of water

❷ a very bad and sad event

❸ 얕은 물: _____ water

❹ happening often

❺ 거대한 고릴라: a _____ gorilla

👇 **Down**

❹ to move along the surface of a liquid

❻ 장엄한 경관: _____ scenery

❼ to prevent something from continuing in the normal way

❽ 똑똑한 아이: an _____ child

❾ 생물학적 기능: _____ function

B   다음 [보기]에서 알맞은 말을 골라 문장을 완성하시오.

> 보기   estimate   offset   abandon   undertake   marine

1   Gains in this area will _____ losses in that area.

2   One of the three companies will be chosen to _____ the project.

3   Plastic pollution is affecting whales, seals, and other _____ life.

4   Because of poverty, he had to _____ his hope of studying further.

5   Experts _____ that the value of the necklace is more than a million dollars.

🔅 생각을 키우는 서술형 · 수행평가 대비 훈련

C   다음 글을 읽고, 밑줄 친 부분 중 어색한 것을 골라 바르게 고치시오.

In 2018, over 170 sea turtles were found dead off the coast of Massachusetts in the U.S. How did these intelligent creatures die? Did they ⓐget lost? Biologists looked for possible causes. ⓑWhat they found explained the tragedy. Like other marine animals, turtles move through the ocean ⓒlooking for food. Before 2010, the area around Massachusetts was too cold for turtles ⓓswim into. But because of global warming, it had become warmer. Then in November 2018, weather conditions suddenly changed. The turtles ⓔgot stuck in cold water and they eventually died.

_____ → _____

Topic Consumer Psychology

언제 어디에서라도 항상 available한 물과 luxury한 다이아몬드 중 우리에게 반드시 필요한 것은? 모든 사람들이 당연히 물이라고 답할 거예요. 물이 없으면 생존에 위협을 받지만, 다이아몬드는 없어도 살 수 있으니까요. 이렇게 모든 사람이 물이 다이아몬드보다 가치 있다고 여기지만 실제로 두 물질의 가격은 정 반대이죠!

왜 생존을 위해 꼭 필요한 물보다 그렇지 않은 다이아몬드가 더 비쌀까요? 이것은 물보다 다이아몬드가 더 scarce하기 때문이죠. 물은 충분한 양을 손쉽게 구할 수 있어요. 반면에 땅속에 있는 다이아몬드의 양은 limited해서, 그것의 demand에 비하면 아주 적은 양만을 supply하는 것이 가능해요. 따라서 다이아몬드의 가격이 increase되어 지금처럼 비싼 것이죠. 만약 다이아몬드가 땅 위를 굴러다니는 돌 만큼이나 흔하다면, 다이아몬드의 가격은 지금보다 훨씬 decrease되었겠죠? 우리가 쉽게 구할 수 없는 상품의 가치가 높게 평가되는 것, 이것을 scarcity의 원칙이라고 해요.

이어지는 지문에는 scarcity의 원칙과 관련된 심리학 이야기와 psychologist들의 재미있는 experiment가 실려 있어요. 과연 어떤 이야기인지 함께 읽어 보죠.

SUPPLY

DEMAND

1 베블런 상품의 가격이 상승하면 수요가 [☐ 감소한다. / ☐ 증가한다.]

106쪽에서 확인

2 우리는 [☐ 구하기 쉬운 물건에 / ☐ 구하기 어려운 물건에] 더 끌리는 경향이 있다.

108쪽에서 확인

☐ 1	**abnormal** [æbnɔ́ːrməl]	형 비정상적인	비정상적인 행동	_____ behavior
☐ 2	**available** [əvéiləbl]	형 이용할 수 있는	이용할 수 있는 공간	_____ space
☐ 3	**consumer** [kənsúːmər]	명 소비자	소비자 운동	a _____ movement
☐ 4	**demand** [diménd]	명 수요	수요와 공급	_____ and supply
☐ 5	**experiment** [ikspérəmənt]	명 실험	과학 실험	a science _____
☐ 6	**influence** [ínfluəns]	동 영향을 미치다	기후에 영향을 미치다	_____ climate
☐ 7	**limited** [límitid]	형 한정된, 제한된	한정된 시간	a _____ time
☐ 8	**luxury** [lʌ́kʃəri]	형 사치의, 고급의	사치품	_____ goods
☐ 9	**participant** [pɑːrtísəpənt]	명 참가자	참가자 목록	the _____ list
☐ 10	**persuasion** [pərswéiʒən]	명 설득	설득의 힘	the power of _____
☐ 11	**psychologist** [saikálədʒist]	명 심리학자	사회 심리학자	a social _____
☐ 12	**rate** [reit]	동 평가하다	영화를 평가하다	_____ the movie
☐ 13	**scarce** [skɛərs]	형 부족한	부족한 자원	_____ resources
☐ 14	**scarcity** [skɛ́ərsəti]	명 희소성, 결핍	물 부족	water _____
☐ 15	**value** [vǽljuː]	명 가치	높은 가치	high _____

어휘 자신만만 QUIZ

1 이런 비정상적인 시장 행동을 베블런 효과라고 한다.

This _____ market behavior is called the Veblen Effect.

2 어떤 것이 희귀할 때, 우리는 무의식적으로 그것이 좀 더 가치 있다고 생각한다.

When something is _____, we automatically think it's more desirable.

🕐 My Reading Time ┃ Words 229 / 2분 33초

1회 ____분 ____초 **2회** ____분 ____초

Everybody knows about the law of demand. When the price of a product goes up, fewer people want to purchase it. When the price goes down, more people want to buy it. It is a common belief that the law works perfectly at all times. However, there are some goods that don't follow this law.

5　　Some kinds of high-status goods, such as designer handbags and luxury cars, are called Veblen goods. Increasing their prices doesn't lead to a decrease in demand. On the contrary, higher prices make the goods more <u>seek</u> after. This abnormal market behavior is called the Veblen effect. It is named after an American economist Thorstein Veblen. He pointed out that some people are willing to pay a higher price, for two

10　possible reasons. For one, many of them believe that a higher price must mean better quality. For another, status-seeking consumers think that the products will help them look special.

However, this market behavior is not completely free from the law of demand. Even Veblen goods are, on some levels, subject to the law. The demand for Veblen goods

15　does not increase infinitely with price. Demand may go up with price until the price reaches a certain limit, but demand will begin to fall if the price goes above its peak. In other words, the law of demand applies _____.

Words

demand 명 수요　　purchase 통 구입하다　　common 형 일반적인, 흔한　　belief 명 믿음　　at all times 항상　　high-status goods 고가품　　luxury 형 사치의, 고급의　　decrease 명 감소　　seek after ~을 구하다, 찾다　　abnormal 형 비정상적인　　behavior 명 행동　　quality 명 질　　consumer 명 소비자　　be subject to ~의 지배를 받다　　infinitely 부 무한히　　peak 명 정점　　apply 통 적용하다

1

What is the main idea of the passage?

a. Abnormal market behavior is unique and not predictable at all.

b. High-status goods are welcomed by many status-seeking consumers.

c. The law of demand applies to high-status goods and everyday goods.

d. Some goods show the Veblen effect, but are partly subject to the law of demand.

• Grammar

2

What is the correct form of the underlined seek?

a. seek   b. seeking   c. sought   d. is seeking

• Inference

3

Which one best fits in the blank?

a. after the peak has been reached   b. contrary to the common belief

c. until the price reaches the peak   d. except the high-quality products

• Graphic Organizer

4

Complete the map using the words from the passage.

If the price goes up   If the price reaches a certain limit

• Some goods show an increase in demand.

• They don't (1)_____ the law of (2)_____.

Veblen Effect

⬆

People believe ...

– a higher price means better (3)_____.

– products of high (4)_____ show their status.

• Veblen goods also start
  to follow the law of
  (5)_____.

스노브 효과(snob effect)

지식백과

스노브(snob)란 우리말로 속물이라는 뜻이다. 스노브 효과는 많은 사람들이 구매하는 물건에 대해서 수요가 줄어드는 현상을 말한다. 자신은 다른 사람들과 다르다는 것을 과시하고 싶은 욕구 때문에 흔하게 볼 수 있는 물건은 구매하지 않으려고 하는 심리 상태를 반영하는 것이다. 베블런 효과처럼, 스노브 효과도 타인이 자신을 어떻게 보는가가 소비에 영향을 미칠 수 있다는 것을 보여준다.

Reading 02

Which Cookie Tastes Better?

⏱ My Reading Time | Words 215 / 2분 23초

1회 ____분 ____초   2회 ____분 ____초

In 1975, psychologist Stephen Worchel did an interesting experiment. A participant was given a chocolate chip cookie from a jar and asked to taste and rate its quality. For half of the raters, the jar contained ten cookies; for the other half, it contained just two. When the cookie was one of the only two available, it was rated more delicious, more desirable and more expensive than when it was one of ten. Why did the participants show different preferences after tasting the same cookies?

This happened because of the so-called "scarcity effect." When something is scarce, we automatically think it's more desirable. On the other hand, we don't set much value on something when it is available everywhere. Therefore, suggesting that a product is scarce or in limited supply is an effective marketing technique. People are more likely to comply with the salesmen's persuasion and buy a product when they think it is scarce. This "available in limited supply" trick shows up everywhere. Special "limited edition" or "last chance to buy" signs are good examples.

Whether we like it or not, we are often influenced by the scarcity effect: we tend to be more attracted to scarce items. But we should be wise enough to know that the scarce cookie doesn't actually taste better.

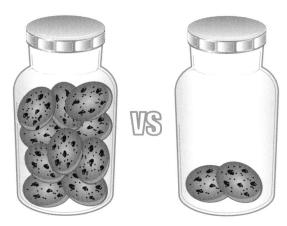

Words　taste 동 ~한 맛이 나다　psychologist 명 심리학자　experiment 명 실험　participant 명 참가자
rate 동 평가하다　contain 동 포함하다　available 형 이용할 수 있는　desirable 형 호감 가는, 가치 있는
preference 명 선호　scarcity 명 부족, 결핍　scarce 형 부족한　set much value on ~을 높이 평가하다
supply 명 공급　comply with 따르다, 준수하다　persuasion 명 설득　influence 동 영향을 미치다

1 • Title

Another title for the passage could be "_____."

a. Who Likes Chocolate Chip Cookies?

b. What Is the Problem of the Scarcity Effect?

c. Why Do People Prefer Scarce Products?

d. How to Set Up an Effective Marketing Plan

2 • Inference

According to the passage, which one attracts consumers most?

a. This is the most loved phone among famous singers.

b. This phone is specially designed for only 500 people.

c. This phone has better functions than any other phone.

d. Everybody has a smartphone now. Why don't you buy one?

3 • Details

Complete the sentences with appropriate words.

When something is in short supply, people think it is more desirable. They are often influenced by the _____ _____.

4 • Summary

Complete the summary with the words from the passage.

A psychologist did an _____. Participants were asked to taste a cookie from a jar and rate its quality. They showed a stronger _____ for what they thought were the _____ cookies. People tend to think a product is more desirable when it is scarce. So, suggesting that a product is scarce is an effective _____ technique. But we should remember that a scarce item is not always _____.

심리학 효과를 이용한 마케팅

심리학이 기업의 마케팅에 활용되는 예로, 구매한 제품과 어울리는 것들을 이어서 구매하는 소비자 심리를 일컫는 '디드로 효과(Diderot effect)'가 있다. 18세기 프랑스 철학자 드니 디드로(Denis Diderot)가 "친구가 붉은 비단 가운을 선물했다. 서재를 가운과 어울리는 분위기로 바꿨지만, 전혀 기쁘지 않았다"고 언급한데서 유래했으며 기업은 브랜드와 관련된 상품을 더 다양하게 개발하려고 노력하고 있다.

▶ 설득의 심리학에 관한 이야기를 동영상으로 만나 보세요. ● Time 1' 40"

A Unit 13에서 학습한 단어를 생각해 보고, 다음 퍼즐을 완성해 보시오.

Across

❶ The meeting room is _____ from 3 p.m.

   (회의실은 오후 3시부터 이용할 수 있다.)

❷ a need for goods and services

❸ done often by many people

Down

❹ 영향을 미치다

❺ worth doing or getting

❻ 참가자 목록: the _____ list

❼ worth of something

❽ 호화 호텔: a _____ hotel

❾ the opposite of normal

❿ 과학 실험: science _____

B 다음 [보기]에서 알맞은 말을 골라 문장을 완성하시오.

> 보기   subject to   demand   scarce   abnormal   comply with

1 The demand for diamonds exceeds the _____ .

2 The company is trying to understand _____ preferences.

3 _____ is to convince someone to do what you want them to do.

4 The man is studying the environmental causes of _____ behavior.

5 Since clean water is _____ in this area, people should walk for an hour to get water.

🔆 생각을 키우는 서술형 · 수행평가 대비 훈련

C 다음 [보기]에서 알맞은 말을 골라 글을 완성하시오.

My brother loves _____ goods, such as designer clothes. To him, if something is expensive or _____ , it is automatically more desirable. Once we went shopping together at his favorite store. It had one brand, just a few items, and one salesperson. When he asked for his size, the salesperson said, "Let me see _____ we have it." He went in the back. Then he came back with one shirt. "Yes, we had it, _____ ," he said. My brother was happy to pay a high price for the shirt, but I think he should be a _____ consumer.

> 보기   scarce   wiser   high-status   if   luckily

#*Topic* Pi(π) & Mathematics

세상에 숫자처럼 **accurate**한 것이 또 있을까요? 우리는 숫자를 사용해서 시간, 거리, 무게, 가격 등을 명확하게 표현할 수 있지요. 그런데 숫자 중에서 **precise**한 값으로 표현할 수 없는 것들이 있다고 하는데 그것이 무엇인지 아나요?

두 정수의 비의 형태로 나타낼 수 없는 실수, 즉, 분수로 나타낼 수 없는 소수를 무리수라고 불러요. 예를 들어, 제곱해서 2가 되는 수인 $\sqrt{2}$는 분수로 나타낼 수 없어요. $\sqrt{2}$를 소수로 나타내면 1.41421356 …과 같이 **endless**한 수가 되죠! 무리수의 값은 정확하게 **calculate**할 수 없어요. 왜냐하면 이들은 무한히 다른 **series**의 수가 이어지기 때문이에요. 여기에는 **repeat** 되는 패턴도 없어서, 우리는 이들의 값을 **estimate**해서 사용할 수 밖에 없죠.

세상에 많이 존재하는 무리수 중 파이(π)는 원의 둘레와 지름의 비율을 나타내는 수학 **symbol**이에요. 우리가 알고 있는 3.14라는 파이의 값은 사실 끝없이 이어지는 숫자에서 **decimal point** 둘째 자리까지만 남긴 거예요. 인공위성을 만든다거나 더 정확한 수를 **figure out**해야 하는 우주 과학 분야에서는 **decimal point** 아래 30자리까지 사용한다는군요. 신기한 무리수 파이(π)에 대해 이어지는 글에서 좀 더 확인해 볼까요?

본문 미리보기 QUIZ

1 첫 번째 파이 데이 기념 행사는
☐ 미국에서
☐ 그리스에서
열렸다.
115쪽에서 확인

2 원주율의 소수점 오른쪽에 연속되는 수는
☐ 반복하지 않는다.
☐ 주기적으로 반복한다.
117쪽에서 확인

독해의 장벽을 깨는 만만한 Vocabulary

Study Date: _____ / _____

☐ 1	**accurate** [ǽkjurət]	형 정확한	정확한 정보	_____ information
☐ 2	**apply** [əplái]	동 신청하다, 적용하다	~에 적용하다	_____ to
☐ 3	**calculate** [kǽlkjulèit]	동 계산하다	비용을 계산하다	_____ the cost
☐ 4	**constant** [kánstənt]	명 상수	수학 상수	a mathematical _____
☐ 5	**decimal point**	소수점	소수점 이하	below the _____
☐ 6	**endless** [éndlis]	형 끊임없는	끝없는 논쟁	an _____ argument
☐ 7	**estimate** [éstəmèit]	동 추산하다	거리를 추산하다	_____ the distance
☐ 8	**figure out**	계산해 내다, 생각해 내다	답을 생각해 내다	_____ the answer
☐ 9	**gather** [gǽðər]	동 모이다, 모으다	자료를 모으다	_____ data
☐ 10	**observe** [əbzə́:rv]	동 기념하다, 축하하다	크리스마스를 기념하다	_____ Christmas
☐ 11	**precise** [prisáis]	형 정확한	정확한 위치	a _____ location
☐ 12	**repeat** [ripí:t]	동 반복하다	그 행동을 반복하다	_____ the act
☐ 13	**series** [síəri:z]	명 연속, 연쇄	일련의 과정	a _____ of process
☐ 14	**symbol** [símbəl]	명 기호, 상징	파이 기호	the _____ for pi (π)
☐ 15	**unofficial** [ʌ̀nəfíʃəl]	형 비공식적인	비공식 언어	_____ language

어휘 자신만만 QUIZ

1 어떤 사람들은 파이 데이는 3월 14일보다는 7월 22일에 기념되어야 한다고 말한다.

Some people say that Pi Day should be _____ on July 22 rather than on March 14.

2 이상하게도, 그 연속되는 수는 결코 반복하지 않는다.

Strangely, the series never _____ itself.

Reading 01 Pi Day

March 14 is a special day in the lives of some people in the U.S. It is Pi Day, an unofficial holiday celebrating the mathematical constant pi (π). The ancient Greek mathematician Archimedes calculated the ratio of a circle's circumference to its diameter, and he found that it was 3.14. _____ Americans write dates in order of
5   month and date, the number 3.14 stands for March 14.

The first Pi Day celebration was held in San Francisco in 1988. _____ then, people around the world have celebrated the day. Usually, they gather and eat pie. One reason why they eat pie is that the words *pie* and *pi* sound the same. In addition, pies come in circles. They discuss how the concept of pi is applied in daily life. Also,
10   they have a contest to see who can say the most digits in pi. Some people even celebrate the so-called Pi Minute. Since pi is 3.14159, the Pi Minute occurs on March 14 at 1:59 am.

However, some people say that Pi Day should be observed on July 22 rather than on March 14. According to them, Archimedes was eventually able to calculate an even
15   more accurate number for pi. Instead of 3.14, he came up with 22/7. On the calendar, they assume, 22/7 or July 22 would be a better Pi Day.

Words

unofficial 형 비공식적인   mathematical 형 수학적인   constant 명 상수   ancient 형 고대의
calculate 동 계산하다   ratio 명 비율   circumference 명 둘레   diameter 명 지름   stand for 나타내다
gather 동 모이다, 모으다   concept 명 개념   apply 동 적용하다   digit 명 숫자   observe 동 축하[기념]
하다   accurate 형 정확한   come up with ~을 떠올리다   assume 동 추정하다

1 • Main Idea

What is the main idea of the passage?

a. Eating pie is an important part of celebrating Pi Day.

b. Archimedes is the mathematician who calculated the value of pi.

c. People observe Pi Day to celebrate the mathematical constant pi.

d. It is important to know how the concept of pi is applied in daily life.

2 • Linking

Which is the best choice for the two blanks?

a. As   b. Because   c. If   d. Since

3 • Details

Complete the sentences with appropriate words.

People eat pie on Pi Day for two reasons. One is that the words *pie* and *pi* _____ the same. The other is that a pie has the shape of a _____.

4 • Graphic Organizer

Complete the map using the words from the passage.

Pi Day: an unofficial holiday celebrating pi (π)		
When	_____ _____	
What people do	• gather and eat _____ • discuss how the concept of pi is applied in _____ life • have a competition to see who can say the most _____ in pi	

How Many Digits Are in Pi?

⏱ My Reading Time | Words 229 / 2분 30초

1회 _____ 분 _____ 초   2회 _____ 분 _____ 초

Everybody knows that the value of pi (π) is 3.14. But do you know where pi comes from? (A) Actually, it comes from nature. (B) In nature, there are circles everywhere: tree rings, flowers, and even eyes. (C) The ratio is always the same, no matter how big or small a circle is. (D) The modern symbol for pi was first used in 1706 by Welsh mathematician William Jones.

Who discovered pi? Nobody knows for sure. The earliest written record of pi dates back to 1900 BC. The Babylonians figured out that pi is about 25/8, while the Egyptians came up with about 256/81. The Greek mathematician Archimedes, who lived in the third century BC, offered 22/7. Pi was estimated by one mathematician after another over thousands of years, and its value was a little different every time. That is so because everyone estimated the value of pi by hand.

With the arrival of the computer, however, it became easier to estimate pi, and the value of pi is more _____ than ever before. Now, the value of pi is 3.14159265.... Unlike numbers such as 3, 9.76, and 10.2387, pi has an endless series of numbers to the right of the decimal point. Strangely, the series never repeats itself. Mathematicians have tried to find a pattern, but they have all failed.

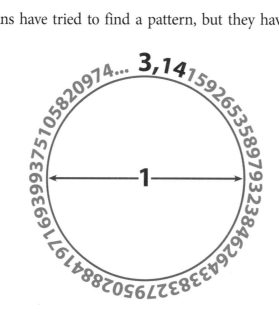

Words value 명 가치, 값   nature 명 자연   modern 형 현대적인   symbol 명 기호, 상징   mathematician 명 수학자   figure out 계산해 내다, 생각해 내다   estimate 동 추산하다   precise 형 정확한   arrival 명 도입, 등장   precise 형 정확한   endless 형 끝없는   series 명 연속, 연쇄   decimal point 소수점

1

Title

Match each paragraph with an appropriate title.

(1) Paragraph 1 •　　　　　• a. The Value of Pi Estimated by Hand

(2) Paragraph 2 •　　　　　• b. More Precise Value of Pi and Its Features

(3) Paragraph 3 •　　　　　• c. The Origin of Pi

2

Organization

Where would the following sentence best fit?

> Pi is the ratio between the circumference of a circle and its diameter.

a. (A)　　　　　b. (B)　　　　　c. (C)　　　　　d. (D)

3

Inference

Which is the best choice for the blank?

a. precise　　　　　b. difficult　　　　　c. inaccurate　　　　　d. shorter

4

Summary

Complete the summary with the words from the passage.

> Pi is the ratio between the circumference of a circle and its _____.
> From 1900 BC, pi was _____ by many mathematicians for a long time,
> and each time the value was a little _____. The arrival of the
> _____ made it easier to estimate pi. Nobody knows the precise value
> of pi because pi has an endless series of numbers to the _____ of the
> decimal point.

지식백과

동양 수학에서의 원주율

고대 동양에서도 정확한 원주율 값을 계산한 바가 있다. 기원전 1세기경 쓰여진 중국 최초의 수학책 「구장산술」에는 원주율의 값이 약 3으로 기록되어 있고, 이후 3세기경 중국의 수학자 유휘는 아르키메데스보다 훨씬 더 정밀한 원주율의 값을 계산해 냈다. 그 후 5세기 후반 송(宋)나라의 조충지와 그의 아들 조항지는 정다각형법으로 원주율의 값이 3.1415926 …이라는 값을 얻어 자신의 저서에 기록하였다. 이는 서양보다 1100년이나 앞선 기록이다.

▶ 수학에서의 '무한대'의 개념에 대한 이야기를 동영상으로 만나 보세요. ● Time 3' 59''

A   Unit 14에서 학습한 단어를 생각해 보고, 다음 퍼즐을 완성해 보시오.

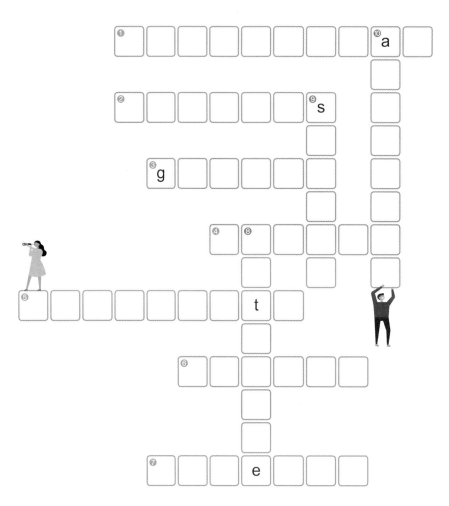

☞ **Across**

❶ the opposite of official

❷ having no end

❸ to bring things together

❹ to say or do something again

❺ 비용을 계산하다: _____ the cost

❻ 행운의 상징: _____ of good luck

❼ to celebrate

👈 **Down**

❽ 추산하다

❾ 일련의 사고들: a _____ of accidents

❿ 정확한 정보: _____ information

B 다음 [보기]에서 알맞은 말을 골라 문장을 완성하시오.

보기	precise	constant	apply	series	observe

1 The law doesn't _____ to this issue.

2 Tim is going to _____ Christmas with his family.

3 Pi(π) is the most widely known mathematial _____.

4 Her calculations were _____ and there were no errors.

5 The professor wrote a _____ of novels related to historical events.

☀ 생각을 키우는 서술형 • 수행평가 대비 훈련

C 다음 글을 읽고, 밑줄 친 부분 중 어색한 것을 골라 바르게 고치시오.

At my school, we celebrate Pi Day on March 14. We make pies, draw circles, and run in circles in P.E. class. But the biggest event is the ⓐcontest. Who can say the most digits? You have to be a little crazy to join ⓑthough you have to sit night after night and try to remember the digits. This year, though, I really wanted to ⓒwin. Up on the stage, I recited 45 digits of pi. Unfortunately, Kevin, last year's winner, recited 58. In the ⓓend, he became King of Pi, while I became Princess of Pi. Everyone ⓔcheered for us, and we each got a prize. It was a pie, of course!

_____ → _____

#Topic Rare Earth Metal & Environment

미국 서부 개척 시대를 배경으로 한 영화에는 종종 황금을 mine하러 가는 사람들에 관한 이야기가 나오곤 해요. 예나 지금이나 금은 사람들이 아주 좋아하는 광물이지요. 그런데 현대 사회에서 금 못지않게 인기가 있고 쓰임새가 다양한 mineral이 황금과 같은 인기를 얻고 있어요. 그 mineral은 바로 희토류랍니다.

희토류라는 말은 사실 우리에게 조금은 낯선 단어일 수 있어요. 하지만 이 광물은 오늘날 high-tech 산업에 없어서는 안될 element예요. 희토류는 우리가 사용하는 휴대전화나 전기 자동차, 반도체 등의 필수 재료거든요. 그런데 global 시장에서 이 희토류의 97%를 중국에서 supply하고 있답니다. 이렇게 valuable한 자원을 독점하다시피 하니 중국의 위세가 아주 대단하겠죠? 한 예로 2010년 중국과 일본 사이에 영유권 분쟁이 있었을 때, 중국이 희토류를 export를 하지 않겠다고 으름장을 놓자 일본은 결국 사과를 할 수밖에 없었어요.

공업용 황금이라고 불리는 희토류의 채광이 언제까지나 낙관적일 수 있을까요? 안타깝게도, 희토류를 캐고 process하기 위해서는 엄청난 환경 오염을 피할 수 없어요. 이것은 희토류가 아닌 다른 광물이나 ore들도 마찬가지죠. 이어지는 글에서는 채광과 환경 오염의 관계에 대해 다루고 있어요. 또 두 번째 지문에서는 희토류에 대해 좀 더 설명하고 있으니, 함께 살펴보도록 해요.

본문 미리보기 QUIZ

1 채광의 큰 문제 중 하나는 [☐ 산성 폐수 / ☐ 대기 오염] 이다.   122쪽에서 확인

2 희토류금속의 종류는 [☐ 17가지 / ☐ 85,000가지] 가 있다.   124쪽에서 확인

☐ 1	**bury** [béri]	통 묻다	씨앗을 묻다	_____ seeds
☐ 2	**concentrate** [kánsəntrèit]	통 집중하다, 모으다	나의 노력을 집중하다	_____ my efforts
☐ 3	**element** [éləmənt]	명 요소, 성분	핵심 요소	a key _____
☐ 4	**export** [ékspɔːrt]	명 수출	수입과 수출	imports and _____ s
☐ 5	**extract** [ikstrǽkt]	통 추출하다	기름을 추출하다	_____ oil
☐ 6	**global** [glóubəl]	형 세계적인, 지구의	세계적인 문제	a _____ issue
☐ 7	**impure** [impjúər]	형 불순한, 더러운	불순물이 섞인 금속	_____ metal
☐ 8	**mine** [main]	통 채광하다	석탄을 채굴하다	_____ coal
☐ 9	**mineral** [mínərəl]	명 광물, 무기질	광물이 풍부한	rich in _____ s
☐ 10	**ore** [ɔːr]	명 광석	철광석	iron _____
☐ 11	**process** [práses]	통 가공하다	우유를 가공하다	_____ milk
☐ 12	**rare** [rɛər]	형 희귀한	희귀한 책들	_____ books
☐ 13	**raw** [rɔː]	형 가공되지 않은	날달걀	a _____ egg
☐ 14	**scatter** [skǽtər]	통 흩어지다, 흩뿌리다	씨를 뿌리다	_____ seeds
☐ 15	**valuable** [vǽljuəbl]	형 소중한, 귀중한	귀중한 교훈	a _____ lesson

어휘 자신만만 QUIZ

1 그것들은 우리가 원하지 않는 불순물도 포함하고 있다.

They also contain _____ elements that we don't want.

2 그것들은 지구 전역에 흩어져 있다.

They are _____ across the globe.

Protect the Environment

⏱ My Reading Time | Words 227 / 2분 30초

1회 _____ 분 _____ 초   **2회** _____ 분 _____ 초

Mining is basically extracting mineral ores from the planet. These ores contain not just the minerals we are looking for. They also contain impure elements that we don't want. So, the extracted ores cannot be used as they are. They need to be carefully processed to get rid of the impurities. This way, we can get valuable minerals like gold,
5 silver, aluminum, salt, diamonds, copper, and even uranium.

By extracting and processing the ores, we get the minerals that serve as the raw materials for various products. With the minerals as raw materials, we can make an almost countless number of products which we use in our daily lives. To name a few, we can make stoves, jewelry, computers, satellites, cars, and even clothing. Without
10 mining, we wouldn't be able to enjoy all the modern comforts.

However, mining offers benefits at a price. One big problem with mining is acidic wastewater from mining operations. Acid water can leak into the nearby soil and watershed, dragging poisonous heavy metals such as lead, zinc, copper, and mercury into the ground and surface water. Mining can also disturb plants and animals. In order
15 to mine, a large piece of land must be cleared. Trees are cut down, and habitats for animals are destroyed. Like many other human activities, mining impacts the environment and therefore must be undertaken with extreme care.

Words	mining 명 채굴, 채광 extract 동 추출하다 mineral 명 광물 ore 명 광석 impure 형 불순한
	element 명 요소, 성분 process 동 가공하다 impurity 명 불순물 copper 명 구리 serve as ~의 역할을 하다 raw 형 가공되지 않은 material 명 재료 countless 형 무수한 satellite 명 인공 위성 benefit 명 이득, 혜택 acidic 형 산성의 wastewater 명 폐수 habitat 명 서식지

1 • Title

Another title for the passage could be "_____."

a. New Ideas for Mining

b. Costs and Benefits of Mining

c. The Minerals as Raw Materials

d. Ways to Extract Valuable Minerals

2 • Words

The underlined impacts means _____.

a. influences

b. develop

c. operates

d. extracts

3 • Details

Which of the following is NOT mentioned as a problem of mining?

a. poisonous wastewater

b. air pollution around mines

c. destruction of forests

d. damage to the animal habitats

4 • Summary

Complete the summary with the words from the passage.

> Mining is _____ mineral ores from the planet and getting rid of the _____ elements from the ores. Minerals from the ores are used as the _____ materials for many products that make _____ life comfortable. However, mining can create one problem after another. First, it pollutes soil and water with _____ heavy metals. It also damages the forests and _____ for wildlife. So, mining must be done with _____.

피의 다이아몬드(Blood Diamond)

결혼식 예물로 흔히 쓰이는 다이아몬드는 변하지 않는 사랑이나 행복을 상징한다. 그러나 어떤 다이아몬드에는 수많은 사람들의 피와 눈물이 얼룩져 있다. 아프리카에는 거대한 다이아몬드 광맥이 존재하는데, 이곳에서 매우 비인권적인 방식으로 채취되는 다이아몬드는 독재자나 군벌의 자본금이 되기 때문에 아프리카에서 불법적인 방식으로 판매되는 다이아몬드를 '피의 다이아몬드'라고 부르게 되었다.

지식 백과

▶ '피의 다이아몬드'에 대한 이야기를 동영상으로 만나 보세요. ⏱ Time 1' 59"

Mining for Minerals · **123**

Reading 02

The Global Race

Nations are racing to have a secure supply of rare earth metals. But why? Rare earth metals are mined for use in such high-tech products as hybrid-car batteries, wind turbines, computer display screens, and medical devices. For example, the rare earth metal Holmium is used to make lasers while Promethium is used to

5 produce nuclear batteries.

There are 17 rare earth metals. They are scattered across the globe, and they are buried in the planet's crust. But rare earth metals are _____ because they are not generally concentrated enough to be economically usable. That is why rare earth metals are called "rare."

10 Highly concentrated ores of rare earth metals are usually found in China. Actually, China is the largest producer of rare earth metals, supplying more than 90 percent of the global

15 market. However, China has been cutting back exports to ensure it has enough rare earth metals for its own use and to protect its environment.

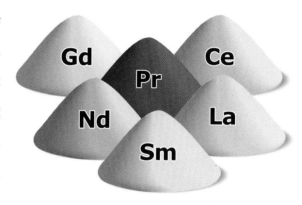

Demand for rare earth metals worldwide, however, grew from about 85,000 tons in 2003 to 125,000 tons in 2008. By 2019, global demand is expected to be

20 1,495,000 tons. Therefore, it may soon be necessary to dig for less concentrated ores of rare earth metals in many countries around the world. If the demand for rare earth metals isn't met, high-tech industries may suffer.

Words
secure 휑 안정된   rare 휑 희귀한   high-tech 휑 첨단 기술의   scatter 동 흩뿌리다   bury 동 묻다
crust 명 딱딱한 표면   concentrate 동 집중하다   economically 부 경제적으로   usable 휑 사용 가능한
cut back ~을 줄이다   export 명 수출(품)

1 · Topic

What is the passage mainly about?

a. the value of rare earth metals

b. the high prices of rare earth metals

c. the rare earth metals produced by China

d. rising demand and shrinking supply of rare earth metals

2 · Inference

Which is the best choice for the blank?

a. not hard to find

b. very difficult to extract

c. fragile to deal with

d. highly concentrated

3 · Details

Complete the sentences with appropriate words.

China has been selling less rare earth metals to other countries. China wants to _____ them for itself and protect its _____.

4 · Graphic Organizer

Complete the map with the words from the passage.

Status

- There are 17 of them.
- They are used to make (1)_____ products.
- (2)_____ is supplying more than 90% of the global market.

Rare Earth Metals

Problem

- China is (3)_____ _____ their exports.
- The international (4)_____ for them is growing.

Results

- Less (5)_____ ores will have to be extracted.
- High-tech (6)_____ may have difficulties.

지식 백과

총성 없는 자원 전쟁 중인 세계

인류의 경제 활동을 위해서는 자원의 공급이 필요하다. 그런데 자원의 양이 제한되어 있어 수요에 비하여 그 공급이 상대적으로 부족한 것을 '희소 자원'이라고 한다. 세계 곳곳에서 희소한 에너지 자원을 두고 주변 국가들 간에 팽팽한 신경전을 벌이기도 하는데, 석유와 천연 가스가 매장된 북극해와 동중국해, 서아프리카 기니 만 등이 그 예이다.

독해의 내공을 키우는 **마무리 학습**

A   Unit 15에서 학습한 단어를 생각해 보고, 다음 퍼즐을 완성해 보시오.

🖝 **Across**

❶ the opposite of common

❷ the minerals that serve as the _____ materials for various products
(다양한 제품에 원자재로 사용되는 광물)

❸ ~으로 고생하다: _____ from

❹ 우유를 가공하다: _____ milk

❺ Oxygen is essential _____ for survival.
(산소는 생존을 위해 필수적인 요소이다.)

Down

❻ 석탄을 채굴하다: _____ coal

❼ 철광석의 수요: demand for iron _____

❽ to put something under the ground

❾ 수출 시장: _____ market

❿ very useful and important

B 다음 [보기]에서 알맞은 말을 골라 문장을 완성하시오.

> 보기   global   scatter   supply   extract   raw

1   We can _____ oil from olives.

2   Soil pollution by heavy metal has become a _____ problem.

3   Farmers often _____ red peppers on a mat to dry them in the sun.

4   The company imports _____ materials and makes finished products.

5   The water _____ system in this area was threatened during a drought.

🔆 생각을 키우는 서술형 • 수행평가 대비 훈련

C 다음 글을 읽고, 밑줄 친 부분 중 어색한 것을 골라 바르게 고치시오.

What happens when high-tech products we use in daily life get old? We ⓐthrow them away, of course. However, there still is a demand for the metals they contain. Some poor people, many of them children, mine through the trash. Then they supply markets ⓑwith the metals. This might ⓒsound good for the environment, but there is a huge human price. The work impacts the children's health. As the children extract the metal parts, they ⓓtouch poisonously materials. This can destroy their health. Hopefully, a better way ⓔcan be found soon.

_____ → _____

생각의 폭을 넓히는 **배경지식** Story

#*Topic* Values & Psychology

행복이란 무엇이고 우리는 어떻게 하면 행복해질 수 있을까요? 이것은 인류가 탄생한 이래로 priest를 비롯한 모든 종교인과 philosopher들이 examine했던 질문이었어요. 긴 논의를 conclude할 수 있는 답은 없겠지만, 20세기 이후 생겨난 긍정심리학은 우리에게 행복해질 수 있는 method에 관한 몇 가지 advice를 제시하고 있어요.

먼저, 긍정심리학자들은 경제적 풍요나 권위가 행복을 보장하지 않는다고 말해요. 이들에 따르면 돈이 항상 우리를 content하게 해 줄 수는 없어요. 경제적으로 풍요롭지만 disappointed한 마음으로 살아갈 수도 있지요. 또한 행복의 중요한 근원은 소중한 사람들과의 관계라고 지적하죠. 먼 미래의 행복을 위해 노력하는 것도 중요하지만, 그렇다고 해서 주위 사람들과의 관계에서 얻는 joy를 소홀히 하지 않아야 한다는 거예요. 뿐만 아니라 행복은 자신의 삶을 의미 있는 일에 사용할 때 얻을 수 있어요. 누군가를 도와줄 때나 힘들지만 보람 있는 일을 할 때 우리는 truly 행복을 누릴 수 있다는 거죠.

어때요, 긍정심리학의 조언이 여러분이 행복을 찾는 데 도움이 될 것 같나요? 이어지는 글은 truly 행복한 사람을 찾는 왕의 이야기예요. 과연 성공할 수 있을지, 함께 읽어볼까요?

본문 미리보기 **QUIZ**

1 항상 행복하지 않은 [☐ 왕이 / ☐ 왕자가] 살고 있었다.

130쪽에서 확인

2 행복한 남자는 [☐ 포도밭에서 / ☐ 사과밭에서] 일하고 있었다.

132쪽에서 확인

☐ 1 **accept** [æksépt] 동 받아들이다 그 제안을 받아들이다 _____ the offer

☐ 2 **comfort** [kʌ́mfərt] 동 위로하다 서로를 위로하다 _____ each other

☐ 3 **conclude** [kənklúːd] 동 결론을 내리다 협상을 결론짓다 _____ the negotiation

☐ 4 **content** [kəntént] 형 만족하는 ~에 만족하는 _____ with

☐ 5 **cure** [kjuər] 동 치료하다, 고치다 병을 고치다 _____ an illness

☐ 6 **disappointed** [dìsəpɔ́intid] 형 실망한 실망한 표정 a _____ look

☐ 7 **examine** [igzǽmin] 동 조사[검토]하다 서류를 검토하다 _____ the paper

☐ 8 **exchange** [ikstʃéindʒ] 동 교환하다 메시지를 교환하다 _____ messages

☐ 9 **harvest** [háːrvist] 동 수확하다 작물을 수확하다 _____ crops

☐ 10 **joy** [dʒɔi] 명 기쁨, 환희 기뻐서 외치다 shout with _____

☐ 11 **method** [méθəd] 명 방법 교수 방법 a teaching _____

☐ 12 **philosopher** [filάsəfər] 명 철학자 현명한 철학자 a wise _____

☐ 13 **priest** [priːst] 명 사제, 신부 사제가 되다 become a _____

☐ 14 **tight** [tait] 형 단단한, 꽉 조이는 단단한 매듭 a _____ knot

☐ 15 **truly** [trúːli] 부 진실로 진실로 놀라운 _____ amazing

어휘 자신만만 QUIZ

1 왕은 이 남자의 셔츠도 그의 아들을 치유할 수 없다고 결론 내렸다.

The king _____ that this man's shirt couldn't cure his son.

2 저는 제가 가진 것에 만족합니다.

I'm _____ with what I have.

Why Are You Unhappy?

There lived a prince who was always unhappy. The king tried to cheer him up with every method possible, but nothing worked.

"Why are you unhappy?" asked the king.

"I don't even know myself, Father."

5 Unable to look at his son's sad face any longer, the king called for philosophers, doctors, and professors to ask for their advice. After examining the prince, the wise men finally said to the king. "You must find a truly happy man, and

10 exchange the prince's shirt for his."

The king immediately sent his men to all parts of the world to look for a happy man. They found a priest and brought him to the king. The king asked the priest, "How would you like to accept a higher position as my bishop?"

"Your Majesty, if only it were so!"

15 The king was _____. He was looking for a truly happy man who would not want more than what he had.

Before long the king's men brought news of the ruler of a neighboring country where people were satisfied in peace. The king visited the ruler and asked what made him so happy.

20 The ruler answered, "Indeed I have everything anybody could possibly want. But I can't sleep at night, worrying about my death and losing all I have accomplished."

The king once again concluded that this man's shirt couldn't cure his son.

Words

cheer up 격려하다   method 몡 방법   philosopher 몡 철학자   professor 몡 교수   examine 통 조사하다, 검토하다   immediately 분 즉시   priest 몡 사제, 신부   position 몡 지위   bishop 몡 주교 Majesty 몡 폐하, 왕   disappointed 혱 실망한   satisfied 혱 만족한   accomplish 통 성취하다 conclude 통 결론을 내리다   cure 통 치료하다, 고치다

• Main Idea

1 What is the main idea of the story?

a. The king tried to find a truly happy man to help his son.

b. The wise men tried to find out why the prince was unhappy.

c. A truly happy man could never be found in the real world.

d. The priest and the ruler were not satisfied with what they had.

• Inference

2 Which is the best choice for the blank?

a. relieved   b. disappointed

c. fearful   d. pleased

• Prediction

3 What would probably happen? Choose one and write your own prediction.

☐ The king couldn't find a truly happy man.

_____

_____

_____

☐ The king finally found a truly happy man.

_____

_____

_____

지식백과

행복한 사람이 더 건강하다!

카네기 멜론 대학의 한 연구진은 긍정적인 감정을 자주 표출하는 사람들과 그렇지 않은 사람들이 감기 바이러스에 노출 되었을 때 병에 걸리는 비율에 대해 연구했다. 놀랍게도, 긍정적인 사람들은 감기 바이러스에 훨씬 적게 감염된 것으로 나타났다. 또한 행복한 사람들은 감기에 걸려도 증상이 더 적거나 약했다. 이 연구 결과는 행복한 감정이 신체의 건강에도 긍정적인 영향을 줄 수 있다는 것을 시사한다.

The king went out to hunt to <u>comfort himself</u>. He heard a man singing a beautiful song from across a field. "Whoever sings like that is bound to be happy!" thought the king.

He finally spotted a young man in a vineyard who was harvesting his grapes.

5 "Good day, your Majesty," the young man said.

"You look so happy today!" the king said.

"Of course, I am happy every day."

"Good. Would you like me to take you to the palace?"

"Much obliged, your Majesty, but I wouldn't change my place for any other

10 place in the world."

"Why not? You can enjoy every kind of comfort at the palace."

"No, I'm content with what I have."

Hearing this, the king shouted with joy. "At last I found a truly happy man! Now my son is saved."

15 The king held the man's hand tight and said to

the man. "Can you do me a favor?"

"With all my heart, your Majesty, if I can."

"My son is dying! Only you can save his life. I'll give you whatever you want. Give me your

20 shirt." The king started to open the young man's jacket.

All of a sudden, the king took a step back. The happy man was not wearing a shirt.

Words

comfort 통 위로하다 명 안락   whoever 누구든 ~하는 사람, 누가 ~하든   be bound to 반드시 ~하다
spot 통 발견하다, 찾다   vineyard 명 포도밭, 포도원   harvest 통 수확하다   content 형 만족하는   joy
명 기쁨, 환희   truly 부 진실로   tight 형 단단한, 꽉 조여 있는   favor 명 호의, 친절   save 통 구하다
whatever 어떤 ~일지라도, 어떤 ~이든

Words

1

What does the underlined comfort himself mean?

a. know himself

b. protect himself

c. make himself happier

d. calm himself down

Feelings

2

When the king opened the happy man's jacket, the king felt _____.

a. surprised

b. happy

b. hopeful

d. relaxed

Details

3

Write T if the statement is true and F if it is false.

(1) _____ The king went out to harvest grapes.

(2) _____ The young man wanted to enjoy the comforts at the palace.

(3) _____ The young man was willing to help the king.

Summary

4

Complete the summary using the words from the passage.

There lived an unhappy prince. The king tried to _____ him up, but nothing worked. The wise men said that the king must _____ the prince's shirt for a truly happy man's. The king found a _____ but he wanted to get a higher position. He talked with the ruler of a neighboring country, but he worried about his _____ and losing what he had. When the king went out to hunt, he finally found a truly happy man. He was _____ with what he had. The king thought the happy man could save his son's life, but the happy man was not wearing a _____.

A   Unit 16에서 학습한 단어를 생각해 보고, 다음 퍼즐을 완성해 보시오.

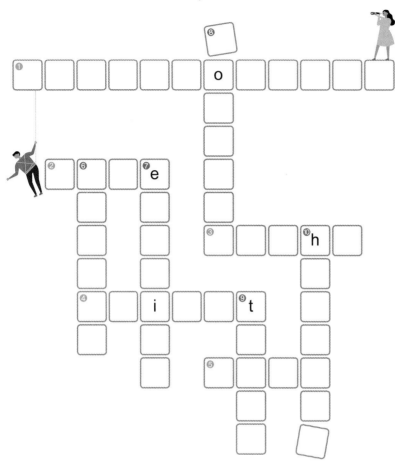

👉 **Across**

❶ unhappy or displeased

❷ 목숨을 구하다: _____ a life

❸ Hold my hand _____.

 (내 손을 꽉 잡아.)

❹ 사제, 신부

❺ to make an illness disappear and someone healthy again

👇 **Down**

❻ the opposite of refuse

❼ The doctor _____(e)d bones of the patient.

 (그 의사는 그 환자의 뼈를 검사했다.)

❽ to make someone feel less worried

❾ 진실로 놀라운: _____ amazing

❿ 작물을 수확하다: _____ crops

B 다음 [보기]에서 알맞은 말을 골라 문장을 완성하시오.

보기	exchange	content	conclude	advice	spot

1 The happy man is _____ with what he has.

2 The debate will _____ at the end of this week.

3 The village people want to _____ eggs for fruit.

4 The police tried to _____ the suspect in the crowd.

5 She offered some useful _____ and encouragement.

🔆 생각을 키우는 서술형 • 수행평가 대비 훈련

C 다음 [보기]에서 알맞은 말을 골라 글을 완성하시오.

I was harvesting my grapes today when a man came up to me. He looked like he had a high position. In fact, he was a king! But he looked unhappy, and he asked me a _____. Naturally, I offered to help him. He told me the story of his son. Then he started to open my jacket to see my shirt. I didn't have _____. The king was surprised and _____. I told him, "I gave my shirt away to a poor _____ this morning." I explained that the _____ to becoming happy is helping others.

보기	favor	one	secret	neighbor	disappointed

Make Your Own Quotes ✏️

앞에서 배운 내용 중에서
마음속에 간직하고 싶은
좋은 문장들을 여기에 적어 봅시다!

I am not sick. I am broken. But I am happy as long as I can paint. (82쪽)

나는 아프지 않다. 나는 부러졌다. 하지만 나는 그림을 그릴 수 있는 한 행복하다.

배경
지식

바로 읽는 독해

바로 읽는 독해

배경 지식

LEVEL 4

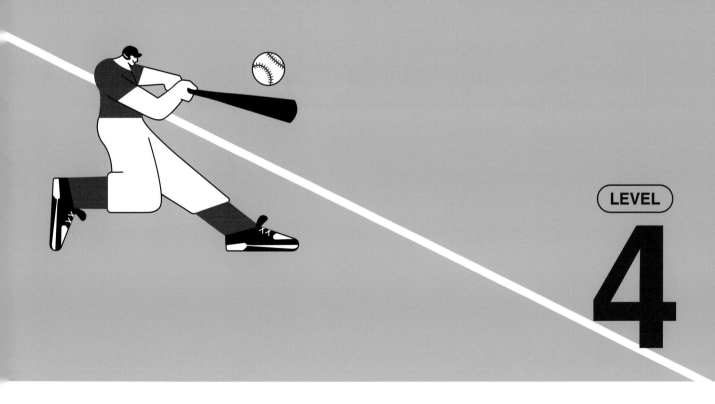

WORKBOOK

CHUNJAE
EDUCATION, INC.

바로 읽는 독해

배경 지식

WORKBOOK

바로 읽는 배경지식 독해

실력향상 WORKBOOK

LEVEL 4

01 Benefits of Olive Oil

쉬운 독해를 위한 Vocabulary 업그레이드

A 다음 영어 표현을 읽고 뜻을 쓰시오.

1	gain		9	prime
2	benefit		10	recognize
3	southern		11	Mediterranean
4	principal		12	in contrast
5	lower		13	according to
6	reduce		14	dietary fat
7	consume		15	heart disease
8	component		16	life expectancy

B 다음 주어진 표현을 배열하여 우리말을 영어로 쓰시오.

1 이들 문화에 있는 사람들은 적은 양의 고기와 유제품을 먹는다.

(small / these cultures / eat / meat / amounts of / people / in / and dairy products)

2 올리브유가 식이지방의 주요 공급원이다. (the principal / olive oil / is / dietary / fat / source / of)

3 어떤 사람들은 매일 아침에 올리브유 한 잔을 마신다.

(a / of / some people / every / drink / glass / olive oil / morning)

4 지중해식 식단은 모든 지방이 나쁜 것은 아니라는 것을 보여준다.

(not / the Mediterranean / fat / is / that / bad / diet / shows / all)

끊어 읽기 구문 학습으로 독해 실력 업그레이드

C 다음과 같이 끊어진 표시에 유의하여 읽고, 문장을 우리말로 해석하시오.

1 The "Mediterranean diet" / gained / worldwide interest / as a model of / healthful eating.

2 People / in this area / — Spain, Greece, and southern Italy — / have / long life expectancy / and / very little heart disease.

3 Many scientists / found / the answer / in their use of olive oil, / a prime component of / the Mediterranean diet.

4 People / of the Mediterranean / have recognized / the benefits of / olive oil.

5 Olive oil / consists mainly of / monounsaturated fat. // It / is / a healthier type / of fat.

6 It / can lower / your risk / of heart disease / by reducing the levels / of bad cholesterol / in your blood.

7 In contrast, / saturated and trans fat / such as butter and animal fat / — increases / your risk / of heart disease.

8 According to / the Food and Drug Administration (FDA), / consuming about two tablespoons of olive oil a day / may reduce / the risk of heart disease.

9 Simply by substituting olive oil / for saturated and trans fat, / you / can have / a healthier diet.

02 **Welcome to Olive Trees**

쉬운 독해를 위한 Vocabulary 업그레이드

A 다음 영어 표현을 읽고 뜻을 쓰시오.

1	deliver		9	relaxed
2	reasonable		10	ingredient
3	memorable		11	substitute
4	delightful		12	commitment
5	produce		13	consistency
6	reputation		14	atmosphere
7	available		15	affordable
8	imported		16	establishment

B 다음 주어진 표현을 배열하여 우리말을 영어로 쓰시오.

1 우리의 목표는 각자의 방문을 유쾌하고 기억에 남을 경험으로 만들어 드리는 것입니다.

(our / each / to / visit / a delightful and / experience / memorable / goal / is / make)

2 이용이 가능한 다양한 선택들을 확인해 보세요.

(choices / out / variety / of / available / check / the wide)

3 우리의 모든 농산물과 빵은 매일 신선하게 배달됩니다.

(all / breads / our produce / fresh / daily / and / are / delivered)

4 우리는 또한 한결같은 맛에 자부심을 갖고 있습니다.

(our / we / also take / in / flavor / consistency / of / pride)

끊어 읽기 구문 학습으로 독해 실력 업그레이드

C 다음과 같이 끊어진 표시에 유의하여 읽고, 문장을 우리말로 해석하시오.

1 Our reputation / for great food and service / has made / Olive Trees / a one-of-a-kind dining establishment.

2 Since 1997, / Olive Trees / has truly been / the best place / to dine / in Starr County.

3 We / take great pride / in serving / our customers / fresh, healthy, fast, and affordable Mediterranean food / in a friendly atmosphere.

4 They / range from / appetizers and salads, / to BBQ chicken and ribs, steaks, seafood, wraps, and kid's meals.

5 We / use / healthy, low-fat, low cholesterol, natural ingredients, / including the best imported olive oil / and low-fat cheese.

6 Our customers / come back again / because they know / they / will always get / good meals / here.

7 Gourmet food / is / not all / that is great about Olive Trees.

8 We / are proud of / our tradition of / serving the best food / in an inviting and relaxed atmosphere.

9 Whether / you are enjoying / a quick lunch with your friends / or a dinner with your family, / our commitment to fine food and reasonable prices / will make / your visit to Olive Trees / special.

01 The Science of Sweat

쉬운 독해를 위한 Vocabulary 업그레이드

A 다음 영어 표현을 읽고 뜻을 쓰시오.

1 cell _____

2 palm _____

3 drenched in _____

4 average _____

5 damp _____

6 effect _____

7 odorless _____

8 stimulate _____

9 fluid _____

10 contain _____

11 evaporate _____

12 excessive _____

13 dehydrate _____

14 unpleasant _____

15 temperature _____

16 get rid of _____

B 다음 주어진 표현을 배열하여 우리말을 영어로 쓰시오.

1 땀은 주로 물과 적은 양의 미네랄을 포함한다.
(a small / sweat / amount / of / contains / mainly water / and / minerals)

2 땀을 흘리는 것은 우리 몸이 열을 식히는 주요한 방법이다.
(is / way / cooling itself / sweating / of / our body's / main)

3 땀은 또한 몸으로부터 노폐물을 제거한다. (of / waste / rid / the body / from / sweat / also gets)

4 여러분이 땀을 너무 흘리면, 여러분은 문제가 생길 수 있다.
(you / into / you / can / if / get / sweat / too / much / trouble)

C 다음과 같이 끊어진 표시에 유의하여 읽고, 문장을 우리말로 해석하시오.

1 Cindy / is about to / make a speech / and / she / notices / that her palms / are damp with / sweat.

2 How can / such different activities / have / the same effect / on the body?

3 Sweat / is produced / in a group of cells / called sweat glands.

4 Sweat glands / are located / over the entire body, / except for / the lips and nipples.

5 When / sweat glands / are stimulated by / physical heat or emotional stress, / a fluid / called sweat / is produced.

6 Sweat itself / is / odorless. // However, / bacteria that feed on sweat / create / an unpleasant odor.

7 When / sweat / evaporates, / it / takes / heat / out of the skin / and / this / helps maintain / the body's temperature.

8 The excessive loss of / salt and water / can dehydrate / the body / and cause / health problems.

9 So, / don't forget to drink / enough fluids / when / you exercise / or stay in high temperatures.

02 **The Birth of Gatorade**

쉬운 독해를 위한 Vocabulary 업그레이드

A 다음 영어 표현을 읽고 뜻을 쓰시오.

1	earn	_____	9	flavor	_____
2	outplay	_____	10	athlete	_____
3	rapidly	_____	11	fatigue	_____
4	replace	_____	12	develop	_____
5	combat	_____	13	well-known	_____
6	opponent	_____	14	worldwide	_____
7	purchase	_____	15	physical activity	_____
8	dehydration	_____	16	muscle cramp	_____

B 다음 주어진 표현을 배열하여 우리말을 영어로 쓰시오.

1 많은 운동선수들이 탈수를 방지하기 위해 그것을 즐겨 마신다.

(many / it / to / to / drink / prevent / athletes / love / dehydration)

2 그것은 피로와 근육 경련을 일으켜, 운동선수들이 최선을 다해 경기를 할 수 없게 한다.

(it / and / keep / can / from / playing / cause / fatigue / athletes / their best)

3 그들은 그 대학교의 풋볼 팀 10명의 구성원들에게 새 제품을 시험하기로 결정했다.

(on / they / to / test / 10 members / of / decided / the university football team / the new product)

4 게토레이에 대한 소유권은 1983년 그 회사가 구입했다.

(Gatorade / purchased / the company in 1983 / to / were / by / the rights)

끊어 읽기 구문 학습으로 독해 실력 업그레이드

C 다음과 같이 끊어진 표시에 유의하여 읽고, 문장을 우리말로 해석하시오.

1 Gatorade / is / a well-known sports drink. // How did / this famous product / get / its name?

2 In the early 1960s, / a team of researchers / at the University of Florida / started / a project / to develop a product / which would combat dehydration.

3 The football coach / recognized / the value of Gatorade / and had / his players / drink / it.

4 The Gators / had / a winning season / and earned / the nickname / "the second-half team."

5 They / outplayed / all their opponents / in the second half of the game.

6 When / an opposing coach / was asked / why they lost, / he replied, / "We / didn't have / Gatorade. // That / made / the difference."

7 Since then, / it / has been / the number one sports drink / in the United States.

8 Now / Gatorade / is produced / in 30 different flavors / worldwide.

9 It / is / the official sports drink of / many American sports leagues, / including the National Football League / and the National Basketball Association.

01 Maps from Long Ago

쉬운 독해를 위한 Vocabulary 업그레이드

A 다음 영어 표현을 읽고 뜻을 쓰시오.

1 carve _____

2 shoreline _____

3 wooden _____

4 accurate _____

5 scale _____

6 apart _____

7 distance _____

8 in short _____

9 traveler _____

10 island _____

11 kayak _____

12 concept _____

13 represent _____

14 marble _____

15 stand for _____

16 figure out _____

B 다음 주어진 표현을 배열하여 우리말을 영어로 쓰시오.

1 믿거나 말거나, 그들 중 많은 이들도 지도를 사용했다.

(or / not / believe / it / also used / it / many / of them / maps)

2 이누이트 지도는 매우 정확했다고 여겨진다.

(it / were / very / that / Inuit maps / is / believed / accurate)

3 고대 로마인들은 지도에 축척의 개념을 더했다.

(the concept / ancient / Romans / scale / maps / to / added / of)

4 축척은 여러분이 지도를 자세히 살펴봄으로써 실제의 거리를 알 수 있도록 해준다.

(scale / lets / in / out / actual distances / by / short / you / figure / examining / a map)

끊어 읽기 구문 학습으로 독해 실력 업그레이드

C

다음과 같이 끊어진 표시에 유의하여 읽고, 문장을 우리말로 해석하시오.

1 For thousands of years, / people / have traveled / to see lands / near and far.

2 How did / the travelers of long ago / find / their way / to new places?

3 Inuits in Greenland, / for example, / carved / wood / to make maps. // The map on the right / has / two pieces of wood.

4 The shorter one / shows / the shoreline, / whereas / the longer one / shows / six islands / close to the coast.

5 Inuits / used / the wooden maps / when / they traveled / at night / by kayak.

6 When / it / was dark, / they / could read / the map / by hand / to find their way.

7 A map's scale / tells / the real distance / that a distance on a map / represents.

8 If / an inch on a map / stands for / 50 miles, / cities / that are 2 inches apart / on the map / are / about 100 miles apart / from each other.

9 A Roman map / was usually carved / in marble, / and / it was placed / on the wall of a public building / so that / everyone / could use / it.

02 Google Street View

쉬운 독해를 위한 Vocabulary 업그레이드

A 다음 영어 표현을 읽고 뜻을 쓰시오.

1 comfort _____

2 display _____

3 launch _____

4 expense _____

5 capture _____

6 misuse _____

7 violate _____

8 convenience _____

9 debate _____

10 location _____

11 visual _____

12 privacy _____

13 access _____

14 millions of _____

15 all kinds of _____

16 have no regard for _____

B 다음 주어진 표현을 배열하여 우리말을 영어로 쓰시오.

1 그것은 사람들이 온라인으로 어떤 곳을 방문할 수 있도록 해준다.

(people / to / online / visit / a location / it / allows)

2 그것은 여러분에게 전 세계의 모든 종류의 장소에 관한 시각 정보를 제공한다.

(gives / it / about / all kinds of / the world / places / around / you / visual information)

3 그것들을 보기 위해서 여러분은 직접 여행할 필요가 없다.

(have to / travel / don't / to see / them / in person / you)

4 이론적으로, 수백만 명의 사람들이 당신의 정원이나 창문을 들여다보는 것이 가능하다.

(into / possible / that / is / millions of people / are looking / in theory / it / your gardens or windows)

끊어 읽기 구문 학습으로 독해 실력 업그레이드

C 다음과 같이 끊어진 표시에 유의하여 읽고, 문장을 우리말로 해석하시오.

1 Google Street View / is / a mapping program / that / provides / people / views of buildings or streets / around the world / at eye level.

2 You / can see / places / in detail / from the comfort / of your home.

3 This is possible / because / Google Street View / uses / a large number of car-mounted cameras / and displays / images of the places / you are interested in.

4 Since / its launch / in 2007, / Google Street View / has been / the subject of hot debate. // Many people / say / that / it / offers / convenience.

5 On the other hand, / there / are / some people / who are deeply concerned.

6 They / think / that / convenience / comes / at the expense of privacy.

7 What you do in private / can be captured / by the cameras, / and anyone / can access / this visual information.

8 It / is likely / that the information / can be misused / by people / who have no regard / for the law.

9 Your privacy / can be violated, / and / even your life / may be / at risk.

01 The Life of the Silkworm

쉬운 독해를 위한 Vocabulary 업그레이드

A 다음 영어 표현을 읽고 뜻을 쓰시오.

1	commonly	9	silk
2	moth	10	tear
3	larva	11	boil
4	mulberry	12	cocoon
5	thread	13	period
6	silkworm	14	hatch
7	insect	15	transform
8	sentence	16	continuously

B 다음 주어진 표현을 배열하여 우리말을 영어로 쓰시오.

1 그 벌레는 작은 알로 자신의 일생을 시작한다. (its / life / as / begins /a tiny / egg / the insect)

2 그것은 이 문장의 끝에 있는 마침표만큼이나 작다.
(at / as / the period / it / is / the end / of / small / as / this sentence)

3 그 알이 애벌레로 부화하기까지 대략 14일이 걸린다.
(days / to / about / takes / fourteen / hatch / into / the egg / a larva)

4 이것은 최상의 비단을 만드는 것을 어렵게 한다.
(it / makes / the / best / this / silk / to / difficult / make)

C 다음과 같이 끊어진 표시에 유의하여 읽고, 문장을 우리말로 해석하시오.

1 Have you ever heard of / the insect *Bombyx mori*? // The name / more commonly used / for this insect / is / "silkworm" / because / it / produces / silk.

2 The larva / then continuously / eats and grows. // It / only eats / the leaves of mulberry trees.

3 At the next stage of its life, / the larva / creates / a cocoon / in about four days.

4 When / it is ready / to make a cocoon, / it / has grown to be / 10,000 times heavier than / when it was an egg.

5 The larva / produces / one long thread / and / covers / its entire body / with it.

6 The cocoon / protects / the silkworm / until / it / transforms / into a moth. // This transformation / takes / about 10 days.

7 If / the moth / comes out / from the cocoon by itself, / it / will tear / most of the thread / into small pieces.

8 To make higher quality silk, / therefore, / the cocoons / must be boiled / before the moths get out.

9 About 3,000 cocoons / are needed / to make a meter of silk, / one of the strongest materials / in the world.

02 The Silk Road

쉬운 독해를 위한 Vocabulary 업그레이드

A 다음 영어 표현을 읽고 뜻을 쓰시오.

1 factor _____

2 branch _____

3 wealthy _____

4 extensive _____

5 luxurious _____

6 middleman _____

7 civilization _____

8 gemstone _____

9 vital _____

10 split _____

11 perfume _____

12 goods _____

13 kingdom _____

14 unbelievably _____

15 be willing to _____

16 trade route _____

B 다음 주어진 표현을 배열하여 우리말을 영어로 쓰시오.

1 실크로드는 세계에서 가장 오래된 무역 경로 중 하나이다.

(is / the world's / of / routes / oldest / the Silk Road / trade / one)

2 그것은 1만 킬로미터 이상으로 뻗어 있다.

(more / it / kilometers / ten / stretches / than / thousand)

3 부유한 유럽인들은 이 사치스러운 옷감에 기꺼이 돈을 지불할 의향이 있었다.

(willing / pay / were / to / Europeans / for / this luxurious cloth / wealthy)

4 물건들은 일반적으로 중간 상인에서 중간 상인으로 넘겨졌다.

(to / from / middleman / goods / were / generally passed / middleman)

끊어 읽기 구문 학습으로 독해 실력 업그레이드

C 다음과 같이 끊어진 표시에 유의하여 읽고, 문장을 우리말로 해석하시오.

1 For more than 14 centuries, / the Silk Road / was / a vital trade route / between Asia and Europe.

2 The Silk Road / was not / a single route, / but / an extensive network of trade routes.

3 The road / started / at Changan, / the capital of the ancient Chinese kingdom.

4 It / continued westward, / connecting one oasis / to another / across Asia's great deserts.

5 It / went through / the Himalayas / and split. // One branch / passed through / Russia / and / was connected to Europe.

6 The road / got / its name from the Chinese silk trade, / which / began / during the Han Dynasty (206 BC – 220 AD).

7 Romans / considered / silk worth / its weight in gold. // Gemstones, perfumes, tea, fine china, and many other items / were also carried / on this road.

8 However, / very few / traveled / the Silk Road / from end to end.

9 Trade on the Silk Road / was / an important factor / in the development / of the great civilizations of / China, India, Egypt, Persia, Arabia, and Rome.

01 The True Value of a Medal

쉬운 독해를 위한 Vocabulary 업그레이드

A 다음 영어 표현을 읽고 뜻을 쓰시오.

1 worth _____

2 host _____

3 unique _____

4 minimum _____

5 guideline _____

6 diameter _____

7 plate _____

8 entirely _____

9 value _____

10 exclusive _____

11 responsible _____

12 at least _____

13 athlete _____

14 compete _____

15 pure _____

16 depend on _____

B 다음 주어진 표현을 배열하여 우리말을 영어로 쓰시오.

1 주최국은 메달을 제작할 책임이 있다.

(responsible / the medals / is / the host country / producing / for)

2 최근 올림픽의 어떤 메달은 더 커졌다.

(been / some / for / medals / recent / larger / have / Olympics)

3 올림픽 금메달은 더 이상 순금으로 만들어지지 않는다.

(Olympic gold medals / longer / pure gold / no / made / are / of)

4 금메달의 가치는 금과 은의 가치에 달려 있지 않다.

(of / doesn't depend on / of / the value / the value / a gold Medal / the gold and silver)

끊어 읽기 구문 학습으로 독해 실력 업그레이드

C 다음과 같이 끊어진 표시에 유의하여 읽고, 문장을 우리말로 해석하시오.

1 Every four years, / athletes from around the world / come together / for the Olympics.

2 But / do you know / who makes the Olympic medals / and / how much they are worth?

3 The host country / can design / the medals / as it wishes.

4 Each medal / must be / at least 60 mm in diameter / and / 3 mm thick.

5 They are / made up of 92.5% silver / and / plated with / at least 6 grams of gold.

6 This is mostly because / it is too expensive to make gold medals / out of pure gold.

7 The last Olympic gold medals / that were made entirely out of gold / were awarded / in Stockholm, Sweden, in 1912.

8 So, how much / is a gold medal / worth?

9 With just 6 grams of gold, / it is worth / no more than about $600.

10 Winning a gold medal / is the dream / of every Olympic athlete.

02 Olympic Sponsorship

쉬운 독해를 위한 Vocabulary 업그레이드

A   다음 영어 표현을 읽고 뜻을 쓰시오.

1   opportunity _____

2   symbolize _____

3   dedication _____

4   achievement _____

5   exclusive _____

6   promotion _____

7   revenue _____

8   contribute _____

9   direct _____

10   confidential _____

11   ideal _____

12   extend _____

13   participate _____

14   sponsor _____

15   advertise _____

16   maintain _____

B   다음 주어진 표현을 배열하여 우리말을 영어로 쓰시오.

1   올림픽 경기에 참가하는 것은 많은 운동선수들의 꿈이다.

(participating / a dream / the Olympic Games / is / many athletes / for / in)

2   그것들은 광고와 마케팅을 위한 최적의 장소 중 하나가 되고 있다.

(have / for / become / one of / they / advertising and marketing / the best places)

3   많은 기업들이 후원 업체가 되기 위해 기꺼이 많은 돈을 지불하려고 한다.

(lots of / be a sponsor / are willing to / to / pay / many companies / money)

4   후원 수익이 올림픽 수입의 40 퍼센트 이상을 차지한다.

(of / revenue / on sponsorship / more than 40% / Olympic revenue / makes up)

C

다음과 같이 끊어진 표시에 유의하여 읽고, 문장을 우리말로 해석하시오.

1   The Olympic Games / provide / great business opportunities / for companies.

2   The Olympic Games / symbolize / youthful energy, dedication and high achievement.

3   Companies / love to / be associated with / these ideals.

4   Sponsors / contribute / cash, products and services.

5   In return, sponsors / receive / the exclusive right / to use the Olympic images / in their advertising and promotions.

6   Without support / from the sponsors, / the Olympic Games / cannot happen.

7   There are / different levels / of sponsorship.

8   TOP partners / must be able to provide / not only cash / but also direct support and know-how for the Games.

9   How much / is needed / to be a TOP Partner / is confidential.

10 The Coca-Cola Company / has supported / every Olympic Games / since 1928.

01 Who Invented the WWW?

쉬운 독해를 위한 Vocabulary 업그레이드

A 다음 영어 표현을 읽고 뜻을 쓰시오.

1 invent _____

2 initial _____

3 address _____

4 connect _____

5 countless _____

6 tool _____

7 organize _____

8 link _____

9 browse _____

10 physics _____

11 laboratory _____

12 develop _____

13 huge _____

14 undoubtedly _____

15 benefit _____

16 contribution _____

B 다음 주어진 표현을 배열하여 우리말을 영어로 쓰시오.

1 어떤 사람들은 월드 와이드 웹이 인터넷과 같은 것이라고 생각한다.

(think / that / the same thing / is / some people / as / the World Wide Web / the Internet)

2 그는 인터넷을 통해 정보를 공유하는 도구를 개발할 필요성을 느꼈다.

(the need / felt / to develop / a tool / information / to share / over the Internet / he)

3 어떤 사람들에게는 그의 업적이 구텐베르크의 인쇄기만큼 중요한 것으로 평가된다.

(as / Gutenberg's printing press / by some / as / is regarded / his work / being as important)

4 그는 어떤 사람도 월드 와이드 웹을 소유할 수 없도록 하기 위해 열심히 싸웠다.

(the World Wide Web / nobody / to make sure / he / that / owns / has fought hard)

끊어 읽기 구문 학습으로 독해 실력 업그레이드

C 다음과 같이 끊어진 표시에 유의하여 읽고, 문장을 우리말로 해석하시오.

1 Most Internet addresses begin with WWW, the initials for the World Wide Web.

2 The Internet is a large network of computers around the world.

3 It connects countless computers in different countries.

4 The World Wide Web is a tool that allows people to organize, link, and browse pages on the Internet.

5 He was born in London in 1955 and studied physics at Oxford University.

6 Thanks to his invention, anyone can get to the huge amount of information on the Internet quickly and easily.

7 Undoubtedly, he could have been rich or famous.

8 He still wants everyone to benefit from his invention.

9 Thus, the tool is free for all, and it will remain so.

10 Berners-Lee was knighted by Queen Elizabeth II in 2004 for his contribution to the world.

02 **Easy Internet Terms**

쉬운 독해를 위한 Vocabulary 업그레이드

A 다음 영어 표현을 읽고 뜻을 쓰시오.

1 term _____
2 enable _____
3 translate _____
4 display _____
5 specific _____
6 indicate _____
7 contain _____
8 path _____

9 particular _____
10 device _____
11 communicate _____
12 consist of _____
13 separate _____
14 dot _____
15 request _____
16 resource _____

B 다음 주어진 표현을 배열하여 우리말을 영어로 쓰시오.

1 웹 브라우저는 우리가 웹 페이지를 읽을 수 있게 하는 소프트웨어이다.

(is / a Web browser / to read webpages / a piece of software / that / enables / us)

2 IP 주소는 인터넷상의 특정한 장치를 나타내는 숫자들로 구성된 암호이다.

(on the Internet / which identifies / made up of / is / numbers / a code / a particular device / an IP address)

3 IP 주소는 0부터 255 사이의 숫자 네 세트로 구성된다.

(from 0 to 255 / four sets of numbers / consists of / an IP address)

4 DNS가 없다면, 우리는 방문하려는 모든 사이트의 IP 주소를 기억해야 할 것이다.

(the IP address of every site / have to remember / would / we / wanted / we / to visit / without DNS,)

끊어 읽기 구문 학습으로 독해 실력 업그레이드

C   다음과 같이 끊어진 표시에 유의하여 읽고, 문장을 우리말로 해석하시오.

1   It / translates the coding language (HTML) / of the World Wide Web / into graphic form / and displays webpages.

2   We can enjoy web surfing / by simply clicking, / without having to know / a coding language.

3   A URL is the address / of a specific website / or a file on the Internet.

4   The first part of a URL / indicates / the type of resource.

5   The second part of a URL / contains / the address of the computer / and path to the file.

6   Every device, / such as a computer or a printer, must have an IP address / in order to communicate / with other devices / on the Internet.

7   It shows / where the device is.

8   DNS is the system / that translates domain names / into IP addresses.

9   When you type in "http://www.google.com," / the computer sends a request / to the nearest DNS server, / which finds the correct IP address for "google.com."

10   Without DNS, / we would have to remember / the IP address of every site / we wanted to visit.

01 **History of Halloween**

A 다음 영어 표현을 읽고 뜻을 쓰시오.

1 celebrate ＿＿＿＿＿＿＿＿＿   9 opposite ＿＿＿＿＿＿＿＿＿

2 costume ＿＿＿＿＿＿＿＿＿   10 soul ＿＿＿＿＿＿＿＿＿

3 holy ＿＿＿＿＿＿＿＿＿   11 haunt ＿＿＿＿＿＿＿＿＿

4 honor ＿＿＿＿＿＿＿＿＿   12 parade ＿＿＿＿＿＿＿＿＿

5 saint ＿＿＿＿＿＿＿＿＿   13 outskirt ＿＿＿＿＿＿＿＿＿

6 religion ＿＿＿＿＿＿＿＿＿   14 treat ＿＿＿＿＿＿＿＿＿

7 custom ＿＿＿＿＿＿＿＿＿   15 soot ＿＿＿＿＿＿＿＿＿

8 originate ＿＿＿＿＿＿＿＿＿   16 primarily ＿＿＿＿＿＿＿＿＿

B 다음 주어진 표현을 배열하여 우리말을 영어로 쓰시오.

1 전 세계의 사람들은 의상을 입고 사탕을 가지고 핼러윈을 기념한다.

(celebrate / people around the world / costumes and candy / with / Halloween)

2 핼러윈의 몇몇 관습은 삼하인이라는 켈트 족 축제에 기원을 두었다.

(originated from / some customs / of Samhain / the Celtic festival / of Halloween)

3 켈트 족은 최근에 죽은 영혼이 이날 밤 지상을 걸어다닐 수 있다고 믿었다.

(the Celts / on this night / that the souls of the recently dead / believed / could walk the earth)

4 어린이들은 오래 전에 켈트 족이 했던 것과 같이 의상을 차려입는다.

(dress up / a long time ago / as / the Celts did / children / in costumes)

끊어 읽기 구문 학습으로 독해 실력 업그레이드

C   다음과 같이 끊어진 표시에 유의하여 읽고, 문장을 우리말로 해석하시오.

1   All Hallows Day / was a holy day / in Christianity / honoring the saints and other people / who had died / for their religion.

2   The Celts / divided the year / into halves: / the light half / and the dark half.

3   The light half / was the time / when the days were longer / and the dark half / was the opposite.

4   Samhain / was held on the day / when the light half ended / and the dark half began.

5   People / didn't want / to be haunted / by unhappy ghosts.

6   So they / would parade / to the outskirts of their villages / and leave sweet treats.

7   They / hoped / that the dead would follow / the parade / and not cause them any harm.

8   These days, / Halloween / is not usually considered / a religious holiday.

9   It is / primarily / a fun day / for children.

10   However, they / don't worry / too much / about evil spirits.

02 **Stingy Jack and the Devil**

쉬운 독해를 위한 Vocabulary 업그레이드

A 다음 영어 표현을 읽고 뜻을 쓰시오.

1	according to		9	trick	
2	miserable		10	flame	
3	cross		11	hollow	
4	promise		12	turnip	
5	remove		13	wander	
6	worthless		14	tradition	
7	Hell		15	replace	
8	toss		16	evil spirit	

B 다음 주어진 표현을 배열하여 우리말을 영어로 쓰시오.

1 그는 모든 사람들에게 장난치기를 좋아하는 고약한 주정뱅이 노인이었다.

(play tricks / was / a miserable old drunk / liked to / who / on everybody / he)

2 Jack은 자신이 죽었을 때 자신의 영혼을 데려가지 않겠다는 약속을 하면 내려오게 해 주겠다고 악마에게 말했다. (he / Jack / told the Devil / when he died / he / his soul / would / let him down / promised / not to take / if)

3 그는 천국에 갔지만 가치 없는 삶을 살았기 때문에 거절당했다.

(had led / he / but / was turned away / a worthless life / he / went to Heaven / because)

4 그들은 그 잭오랜턴(jack-o' lantern)을 Jack과 다른 악령들이 가까이 올 수 없게 문간에 놓았다.

(away / they / a jack-o' lantern / to keep / on their doorsteps / Jack and other evil spirits / left)

C

다음과 같이 끊어진 표시에 유의하여 읽고, 문장을 우리말로 해석하시오.

1 According to / Irish folklore, / there once lived a man / named Stingy Jack.

2 One day, / he / tricked the Devil / into / climbing an apple tree / and then planted crosses / around the tree.

3 The Devil / couldn't get down.

4 When / the Devil agreed, / Jack / removed all the crosses / and let the Devil down.

5 So, / then / he / went down / to Hell.

6 The Devil / kept his promise / and / didn't let him in.

7 Jack / now had nowhere / to go.

8 He / asked the Devil / how he could see / where to go / with no light.

9 The Devil / tossed / him / an ember / from the flames of Hell.

10 On All Hallows Eve, / the Irish / hollowed out turnips / and placed lights / inside them.

01 Greenland Is Not Green

쉬운 독해를 위한 Vocabulary 업그레이드

A 다음 영어 표현을 읽고 뜻을 쓰시오.

1 mistakenly _____

2 nation _____

3 climate _____

4 self-governing _____

5 province _____

6 population _____

7 contrary to _____

8 area _____

9 settler _____

10 exile _____

11 murder _____

12 attract _____

13 colonization _____

14 densely _____

15 mild _____

16 be covered with _____

B 다음 주어진 표현을 배열하여 우리말을 영어로 쓰시오.

1 그린란드는 세계에서 가장 큰 섬이다.

(Greenland / the world's / is / island / largest)

2 그린란드라는 이름은 초기 스칸디나비아 정착민들로부터 유래한다.

(Scandinavian settlers / Greenland / comes from / the name / the early)

3 덴마크의 식민지 건설이 시작된 것은 18세기가 되어서였다.

(it / Danish colonization / that / only / began / in the 18th century / was)

4 그린란드는 여전히 세계에서 인구밀도가 가장 낮은 곳이다.

(densely populated place / in the world / still / the least / remains / Greenland)

C 다음과 같이 끊어진 표시에 유의하여 읽고, 문장을 우리말로 해석하시오.

1 Some people / mistakenly / think / that it is a nation.

2 Greenland / lies / just south of the Arctic Circle, / so / it is very cold / there.

3 In the winter months, / the temperatures / are below freezing / all day long.

4 Contrary to / its name, / most areas of Greenland / are covered with / ice.

5 He / named the island Greenland, / hoping / that the good name / would attract / other settlers.

6 Greenland is 2.1 million km^2, / which means / it is ten times / as big as / the Korean Peninsula.

7 Around 90% / of the population / is Inuit or mixed Danish and Inuit.

8 The rest / are from European origins, / mainly Danish.

9 Nearly all Greenlanders / live in the southwest / of the main island, / which has a relatively mild climate.

10 More than 25% of the population / lives / in the capital, Nuuk.

UNIT 08

02 Continent or Island?

쉬운 독해를 위한 Vocabulary 업그레이드

A 다음 영어 표현을 읽고 뜻을 쓰시오.

1 continent _____

2 status _____

3 separate _____

4 criteria _____

5 tectonically _____

6 independent _____

7 biological _____

8 scientific _____

9 local _____

10 subjective _____

11 distinct _____

12 wildlife _____

13 similar _____

14 unique _____

15 official _____

16 classify _____

B 다음 주어진 표현을 배열하여 우리말을 영어로 쓰시오.

1 그린란드는 섬으로 알려져 있는 반면 오스트레일리아는 대륙으로 여겨진다.

(considered / Greenland / as / while / Australia / is known / is / an island / a continent)

2 다른 대륙과 지질구조상 독립되어야 한다.

(other continents / it / tectonically / must be / from / independent)

3 독특한 동물과 식물체가 있는 생물학적 특수성이 있어야 한다.

(biological distinctiveness / it / unique / must have / animal and plant life / with)

4 그린란드의 야생 동물은 북아메리카의 야생동물들과 거의 비슷하다.

(that of North America's / Greenland's wildlife / largely / similar to / is)

끊어 읽기 구문 학습으로 독해 실력 업그레이드

C 다음과 같이 끊어진 표시에 유의하여 읽고, 문장을 우리말로 해석하시오.

1 It appears / they / should have / the same status.

2 To be a continent, / a piece of land / should meet / four criteria.

3 It / must have / unique cultures.

4 Local people / must believe it / to be a continent.

5 The first two / are scientific, / whereas / the second two / are more subjective.

6 The table above / shows / why Australia is a continent / while / Greenland is an island.

7 Australia / sits on / its own tectonic plate / whereas / Greenland is / geologically part of North America.

8 Australia / has / highly distinct plants and animals.

9 Greenland / even has / its own official language, / Greenlandic.

10 However, / their cultures / can be classified as / part of a larger North American culture.

01 Why a Gap Year?

쉬운 독해를 위한 Vocabulary 업그레이드

A 다음 영어 표현을 읽고 뜻을 쓰시오.

1 pursue _____

2 opportunity _____

3 origin _____

4 benefit _____

5 acquire _____

6 convince _____

7 encourage _____

8 prestigious _____

9 option _____

10 concept _____

11 momentum _____

12 motivate _____

13 essential _____

14 take time off _____

15 volunteer work _____

16 a rite of passage _____

B 다음 주어진 표현을 배열하여 우리말을 영어로 쓰시오.

1 그들은 다양한 용도로 이 시간을 활용한다. (use / this / they / different / purposes / time / for)

2 갭이어 경험은 몇 주 혹은 일 년까지 지속될 수도 있다.
(year / last / a full year / weeks / or / up to / experience / can / a gap / for / several)

3 그들은 자신에 대해 발견할 수 있는 기회를 가진다.
(get / to / find / about / a chance / themselves / they / out)

4 그 개념은 영국에 기원을 둔다. (has / its / origins / in / the / concept / the United Kingdom)

끊어 읽기 구문 학습으로 독해 실력 업그레이드

C 다음과 같이 끊어진 표시에 유의하여 읽고, 문장을 우리말로 해석하시오.

1 Many young people / in English-speaking countries / take time off / before / they / start / university.

2 While / some / travel / or / pursue their hobbies, / many / enjoy / doing volunteer work, / often abroad.

3 In the past, / only a small number of students / could take / a gap year. // The idea of a gap year / gained / momentum / in the 1990s.

4 Since then, / taking time out / has become / a rite of passage / for tens of thousands of / U.K. students.

5 Does / this time off / help / the "gappers"? // Research / says / that it does.

6 Students who take a gap year / are more focused / and motivated / when / they start to study / at college.

7 A gap year / gives / them / the opportunity / to learn about the real world / and acquire / essential life skills.

8 For these reasons, / some of the most prestigious universities / are convinced of / the benefits of a gap year.

9 Harvard University, / for instance, / encourages / every new freshman / to consider / taking the option seriously.

02 A Year in Kenya

쉬운 독해를 위한 Vocabulary 업그레이드

A 다음 영어 표현을 읽고 뜻을 쓰시오.

1 horrible _____

2 install _____

3 diarrhea _____

4 school supply _____

5 instructional _____

6 cuisine _____

7 food poisoning _____

8 equipment _____

9 valuable _____

10 dreadful _____

11 look back _____

12 plenty of _____

13 deal with _____

14 suffer from _____

15 reflect on _____

16 set foot _____

B 다음 주어진 표현을 배열하여 우리말을 영어로 쓰시오.

1 돌이켜 보면, 케냐에서의 모든 것이 아주 좋았다.

(Kenya / has been / I / look / when / in / back / everything / great)

2 새 우물은 모든 아이들에게 깨끗한 물을 제공할 것이다.

(clean / well / water / to / will / give / every / the new / kid)

3 나는 다른 사람들을 돕는 것이 나를 행복하게 한다는 것을 배웠다.

(makes / that / I / helping / me / learned / others / happy)

4 나는 지역 문화와 요리법에 관하여 배울 수 있는 많은 기회를 얻었다.

(I / to / had / of / and / cuisine / opportunities / learn about / the local / culture / plenty)

끊어 읽기 구문 학습으로 독해 실력 업그레이드

C 다음과 같이 끊어진 표시에 유의하여 읽고, 문장을 우리말로 해석하시오.

1 It / has been / nearly a year / since / I / first set foot / in Kenya / to spend my gap year.

2 So far, / I / haven't suffered from / any really dreadful diseases / that / the locals / have to deal with.

3 This afternoon, / I / had / terrible diarrhea, / perhaps because of food poisoning.

4 Thanks to some herbal medicine, / however, / I / feel better now / and / ready to reflect on / what has happened here / over the past year.

5 Books and other school supplies / arrived, / new desks and chairs / were brought / into the building, / and / high-tech instructional equipment / was also installed / in every classroom.

6 The kids from the village / will soon study / in better classrooms / and take breaks / on a safer playground.

7 I / am proud / that / I / could be of help / to the kids here.

8 I / didn't know / that / a gap year in Africa / would teach / me / so many valuable lessons.

9 Tomorrow / will be / my last day / in Kenya, / and / I / will miss / everything here, / except the horrible diarrhea.

01 A Woman of Amazing Strength

쉬운 독해를 위한 Vocabulary 업그레이드

A 다음 영어 표현을 읽고 뜻을 쓰시오.

1 pain _____
2 highly _____
3 physical _____
4 injure _____
5 destroy _____
6 theme _____
7 well-known _____
8 strength _____

9 amazing _____
10 regard _____
11 emotional _____
12 control _____
13 self-portrait _____
14 despite _____
15 operation _____
16 as long as _____

B 다음 주어진 표현을 배열하여 우리말을 영어로 쓰시오.

1 나는 그림을 그릴 수 있는 한 행복하다. (long / as / am / happy / I / can / I / as / paint)

2 그녀의 의사는 그녀가 살아날 거라는 것을 기대하지 않았다.
   (expect / to / her doctor / didn't / her / survive)

3 그녀의 그림들은 단순히 그녀에게 무엇이 일어났는지를 보여준다.
   (what / simply show / happening / her / paintings / to / was / her)

4 그녀의 삶에서의 모든 고통에도 불구하고 그녀는 계속해서 그림을 그렸다.
   (all / to / her life / she / despite / continued / the pain / in / paint)

끊어 읽기 구문 학습으로 독해 실력 업그레이드

C 다음과 같이 끊어진 표시에 유의하여 읽고, 문장을 우리말로 해석하시오.

1 It / was / Frida Kahlo. // She / is / a well-known Mexican painter / whose works of art / are / highly regarded / around the world.

2 Although / her life / was filled with / physical and emotional pain, / she / never allowed / it / to take control of her.

3 Frida Kahlo / was born / in 1907 in Coyoacan, Mexico. // At six, / she / suffered from polio.

4 At 18, / she / was injured / in a car accident, / and her body / was almost destroyed.

5 She / had to have / 35 operations / and / was never able to / have a baby.

6 It was / during her stay in hospital / that / Frida Kahlo / began to paint.

7 Her works / show / the events in her life, / her emotions, / and the changes in her feelings.

8 Pain / is / a common theme / in her works, / which are often violent-looking and bloody.

9 Her paintings / are / the most honest expressions / of herself.

02 The Art of Painting Oneself

쉬운 독해를 위한 Vocabulary 업그레이드

A   다음 영어 표현을 읽고 뜻을 쓰시오.

1 trend _____

2 depict _____

3 canvas _____

4 exploration _____

5 jewelry _____

6 reveal _____

7 famous _____

8 professional _____

9 appearance _____

10 elsewhere _____

11 reality _____

12 therapy _____

13 crippled _____

14 mentally _____

15 troubling _____

16 pay for _____

B   다음 주어진 표현을 배열하여 우리말을 영어로 쓰시오.

1 자화상은 화가들이 그들 자신을 그린 그림이다.

(are / pictures / paint / self-portraits / of / themselves / artists)

2 자화상은 아주 오래 전부터 만들어져 왔다.

(been / since / self-portraits / have / the earliest / made / times)

3 그는 좀처럼 정면으로 우리를 보지 않는다. (at / he / directly / seldom / looks / us)

4 그녀는 그녀의 캔버스 위에 그녀의 감정들을 드러낸다.

(on / she / her / lets out / canvases / her feelings)

C 다음과 같이 끊어진 표시에 유의하여 읽고, 문장을 우리말로 해석하시오.

1   With the appearance / of better and cheaper mirrors, / artists / could easily model / for their own works of art.

2   He / may have painted / so many self-portraits / because / he / didn't have / enough money / to pay for a professional model.

3   He / usually looks / elsewhere. // His self-portraits / depict / his face / as it appeared / in the mirror.

4   So, / his right side in the picture / is / in reality / the left side of his face.

5   The story of Frida Kahlo, / another artist / known for painting herself, / can be read / in her self-portraits.

6   About one-third of her work / is / the exploration of herself, / physically and mentally.

7   Kahlo / created / 55 self-portraits / as a kind of therapy / to face the most troubling events / in her life.

8   In reality, / she / wore / a long dress / and covered herself / with jewelry / to hide her crippled leg and broken body.

9   In her self-portraits, / however, / she / comes out from hiding / and / reveals her pain.

01 Pluto and Eris

쉬운 독해를 위한 Vocabulary 업그레이드

A 다음 영어 표현을 읽고 뜻을 쓰시오.

1	status	9	orbit
2	criteria	10	gravity
3	dwarf	11	definition
4	stable	12	massive
5	planet	13	immediate
6	intensify	14	reclassify
7	approximately	15	diameter
8	dominant	16	solar system

B 다음 주어진 표현을 배열하여 우리말을 영어로 쓰시오.

1 명왕성은 행성으로서의 지위를 잃었다. (status / as / Pluto / lost / a / its / planet)

2 명왕성은 다른 여덟 개의 행성보다 훨씬 더 작았다.

   (eight / Pluto / smaller / was / much / than / planets / the other)

3 그 이름은 발견한 팀에 의해 제안되었다.

   (by / the / was / proposed / discovery / team / the name)

4 Eris는 자신의 가장 큰 즐거움이 분쟁을 일으키는 것인 그리스의 여신이다.

   (to / Eris / joy / whose / greatest / trouble / is / Greek / make / is / the / goddess)

끊어 읽기 구문 학습으로 독해 실력 업그레이드

C 다음과 같이 끊어진 표시에 유의하여 읽고, 문장을 우리말로 해석하시오.

1 From its discovery in 1930 / until 2006, / Pluto / was considered / the solar system's ninth planet.

2 Under the new IAU definition of a planet, / however, / Pluto / no longer meets / the criteria / and / was reclassified / as a dwarf planet.

3 A planet / is / any object in orbit around the Sun / with a diameter greater than 2,000 km, / whose shape is stable / due to its own gravity, / that is dominant / in its immediate neighborhood.

4 So / there had been / a long debate / about whether / Pluto / was / a planet or not.

5 The debate / had intensified / after the discovery of a massive object, / called 2003 UB313, in 2005.

6 It / is / approximately 2,300 kilometers / in diameter / and / a little larger / than Pluto.

7 At first, / it / was discussed / whether / the newly-discovered object / would be / the tenth planet.

8 At the 2006 IAU meeting, / however, / it / was also classified / as a dwarf planet, / along with Pluto. // They / were not dominant / in their neighborhood.

9 The name Eris / is / a perfect fit / for the object / considering / it brought about one of the largest debates / in the astronomical community.

02 The Trojan War

쉬운 독해를 위한 Vocabulary 업그레이드

A 다음 영어 표현을 읽고 뜻을 쓰시오.

1 sail _____

2 discord _____

3 ownership _____

4 wisdom _____

5 legendary _____

6 mythology _____

7 celebrate _____

8 soldier _____

9 except _____

10 claim _____

11 proclaim _____

12 outraged _____

13 hollow _____

14 deceive _____

15 trophy _____

16 belong to _____

B 다음 주어진 표현을 배열하여 우리말을 영어로 쓰시오.

1 그녀는 그 사과가 가장 아름다운 이의 것이라고 말했다.

(the apple / to / she / said / the / belonged / fairest)

2 그는 스파르타로 떠나서 헬렌을 트로이로 데려왔다.

(for / Sparta / took / he / left / Helen / to / and / Troy)

3 그것이 어떻게 그 전설적인 전쟁이 시작되었는지에 관한 것이다.

(how / that / is / war / the / legendary / started)

4 나머지 그리스 사람들은 트로이 사람들을 속이기 위해 배를 타고 떠났다.

(deceive / of / rest / sailed / away / to / the / the Greeks / the Trojans)

C

끊어 읽기 구문 학습으로 독해 실력 업그레이드

다음과 같이 끊어진 표시에 유의하여 읽고, 문장을 우리말로 해석하시오.

1 All the gods / were invited / to their wedding / except Eris, / the goddess of discord.

2 The angry goddess / turned up anyway / and threw / a golden apple / onto the table.

3 Zeus / proclaimed / that Paris, / prince of Troy, / would act / as the judge.

4 Hera / promised / him / power, / Athena / promised / him / wisdom and skill in war, / and Aphrodite / promised / him / the most beautiful woman.

5 Menelaus / was outraged / and asked / other Greek kings / to join the war / against Troy.

6 Nine years / after the war broke out, / the Greeks / still couldn't break down / the walls of Troy.

7 Odysseus / ordered / Greek soldiers / to build a large wooden horse / which was hollow.

8 Once / the statue / was built, / Odysseus and some soldiers / hid / inside of it.

9 The Trojans / thought / the Greeks had left / and / celebrated their victory.

10 That night, / after / most of Troy / had fallen asleep, / the Greek soldiers / came down from the horse / and attacked.

01 Whales on the Beach

쉬운 독해를 위한 Vocabulary 업그레이드

A 다음 영어 표현을 읽고 뜻을 쓰시오.

1 pod _____

2 navy _____

3 shallow _____

4 helpless _____

5 disrupt _____

6 shore _____

7 intelligent _____

8 magnetic _____

9 trap _____

10 strand _____

11 majestic _____

12 theory _____

13 tragedy _____

14 abandon _____

15 frequent _____

16 anomaly _____

B 다음 주어진 표현을 배열하여 우리말을 영어로 쓰시오.

1 그것은 비극이고, 우리는 왜 그것이 일어나는지를 알지 못한다.

(why / it / is / and / it / we / know / a tragedy / don't / happens)

2 과학자들은 여전히 이 수수께끼를 풀 수 있는 단서들을 찾고 있다.

(are / that / still searching / scientists / this / mystery / for clues / will / unlock)

3 고래가 얕은 물로 헤엄쳐 오는 이유에 관한 몇 가지 이론이 있다.

(are / whales / into / shallow / some / swim / there / theories / about / why / water)

4 그들은 한 아픈 고래를 돕기 위해 해안으로 따라와서, 갇히게 된다.

(they / shore / to help it / and / follow / become / a sick whale / on / stuck)

끊어 읽기 구문 학습으로 독해 실력 업그레이드

C 다음과 같이 끊어진 표시에 유의하여 읽고, 문장을 우리말로 해석하시오.

1 In February 2011, / a pod of 107 whales / was found / beached / on Stewart Island, / New Zealand.

2 A few weeks earlier, / on the coast of South Island / in New Zealand, / a pod of 80 pilot whales / had been found.

3 Today there are / still frequent reports of whales / lying helpless / and dying / on the beach.

4 How / do / some of the most intelligent animals / get stranded / on the beach / in many parts of the world?

5 As / whales / are very social, / the other healthy whales / refuse to abandon / their sick friend.

6 Another theory / is related to / navy sonar, / which is a measuring technique / using sound and echoes.

7 Some scientists / say / that the low-frequency and mid-frequency sonar / used by navies / can disrupt / an animal's navigation system, / causing it to lose its way, / stray into shallow water, / and end up trapped / on the beach.

8 Besides / the above two most common theories, / there / are / other possible causes, / which include / weather conditions, / magnetic field anomalies, / diseases, etc.

9 Whatever / the cause / may be, / it / wouldn't be easy / to stop / the mass strandings of / these majestic creatures.

02 Awesome Whale Poop

쉬운 독해를 위한 Vocabulary 업그레이드

A 다음 영어 표현을 읽고 뜻을 쓰시오.

1 roughly _____

2 offset _____

3 undertake _____

4 minute _____

5 eventually _____

6 mammal _____

7 biological _____

8 atmosphere _____

9 livestock _____

10 squid _____

11 marine _____

12 stimulate _____

13 estimate _____

14 biologist _____

15 population _____

16 carbon dioxide _____

B 다음 주어진 표현을 배열하여 우리말을 영어로 쓰시오.

1 그들은 바다로 깊이 잠수하는데, 그곳에서 오징어를 먹고 산다.

(where / they / feed / dive deep / on / they / in / the ocean / squid)

2 그들은 숨을 쉬기 위해 수면으로 되돌아온다.

(back / come / to / breathe / to / the surface / they)

3 그것은 철분이 풍부하기 때문에, 플랑크톤의 성장을 촉진하는 데 도움을 준다.

(is / iron / it / helps / stimulate / because / in / plankton growth / it / rich)

4 이것은 이산화탄소의 양과 같다. (the / amount / of / this / is / to / carbon dioxide / equal)

끊어 읽기 구문 학습으로 독해 실력 업그레이드

C 다음과 같이 끊어진 표시에 유의하여 읽고, 문장을 우리말로 해석하시오.

1 Here on land, / we / undertake / great engineering projects / to get rid of / biological waste / from cities and livestock farms.

2 What about / the sea, / where / huge animals / produce / a lot of waste?

3 A recent study / suggests / that / sperm whales in the Southern Ocean / have / the ability / to offset greenhouse gases / with their poop.

4 Whale poop / pulls / carbon dioxide / from the atmosphere / and / moves / it / to the bottom of the ocean.

5 The whale poop / showers over / minute plants / floating on the surface.

6 The plankton / take in / carbon dioxide / from the atmosphere / and eventually sink / to the bottom of the ocean.

7 These ocean giants / and certain other marine mammals / may, / therefore, / be among / the most environmentally friendly animals / on the planet.

8 According to the researchers, / one sperm whale / can take care of / roughly 200,000 tons of carbon dioxide / a year.

9 If / whale poop / indeed cleans / the environment, / shouldn't we / make sure that / whales / are protected?

01 The Veblen Effect

쉬운 독해를 위한 Vocabulary 업그레이드

A 다음 영어 표현을 읽고 뜻을 쓰시오.

1 purchase _____

2 common _____

3 belief _____

4 luxury _____

5 decrease _____

6 abnormal _____

7 quality _____

8 behavior _____

9 at all times _____

10 high-status goods _____

11 be subject to _____

12 seek after _____

13 demand _____

14 perfectly _____

15 increase _____

16 influence _____

B 다음 주어진 표현을 배열하여 우리말을 영어로 쓰시오.

1 이 법칙이 항상 완벽하게 작용한다는 것이 일반적인 생각이다.

(it is / that / the law / at all times / a common belief / works perfectly)

2 이 상품들의 가격 상승은 수요의 감소로 이어지지 않는다.

(a decrease / increasing / doesn't lead / in demand / their prices / to)

3 높은 지위를 추구하는 소비자들은 그 상품들이 자신들을 특별하게 보이게 도와줄 것이라고 생각한다.

(think / look special / that / the products / them / help / will / status-seeking consumers)

4 정점에 이른 이후에는 수요의 법칙이 적용된다.

(has been / the law of demand / the peak / after / reached / applies)

C 다음과 같이 끊어진 표시에 유의하여 읽고, 문장을 우리말로 해석하시오.

1 When / the price of a product / goes up, / fewer people / want to / purchase it.

2 When / the price / goes down, / more people / want to buy it.

3 However, / there are / some goods / that don't follow / this law.

4 Some kinds of / high-status goods, / such as designer handbags and luxury cars, / are called / Veblen goods.

5 On the contrary, / higher prices / make the goods / more sought after.

6 This abnormal market behavior / is called / the Veblen effect.

7 It is / named after / an American economist Thorstein Veblen.

8 He / pointed out / that some people / are willing to pay a higher price, / for two possible reasons.

9 For one, / many of them / believe that a higher price / must mean better quality.

10 However, / this market behavior / is not completely free from / the law of demand.

02 Which Cookie Tastes Better?

쉬운 독해를 위한 Vocabulary 업그레이드

A 다음 영어 표현을 읽고 뜻을 쓰시오.

1	psychologist	_____	9	value	_____
2	experiment	_____	10	supply	_____
3	rate	_____	11	persuasion	_____
4	available	_____	12	comply with	_____
5	desirable	_____	13	participant	_____
6	preference	_____	14	taste	_____
7	scarcity	_____	15	influence	_____
8	scarce	_____	16	contain	_____

B 다음 주어진 표현을 배열하여 우리말을 영어로 쓰시오.

1 왜 참가자들은 같은 과자를 맛본 후에 다른 선호도를 보였을까? (did / the participants / tasting / different preferences / why / after / show / the same cookies / ?)

2 이것은 소위 말하는 '희소성 효과' 때문이었다.
("scarcity effect" / because of / happened / the so-called / this)

3 제품이 희귀하다고 말하는 것은 효과적인 마케팅 기법이다.
(marketing technique / suggesting / is / is / that / scarce / an effective / a product)

4 우리는 희소한 물건에 더 끌리는 경향이 있다.
(scarce items / we / be / more attracted / tend to / to)

끊어 읽기 구문 학습으로 독해 실력 업그레이드

C 다음과 같이 끊어진 표시에 유의하여 읽고, 문장을 우리말로 해석하시오.

1 In 1975, / psychologist Stephen Worchel / did an interesting experiment.

2 A participant / was given / a chocolate chip cookie / from a jar / and / asked to / taste and rate its quality.

3 For half of the raters, / the jar / contained / ten cookies; / for the other half, / it / contained / just two.

4 When / something is scarce, / we / automatically think / it's more desirable.

5 On the other hand, / we / don't set much value / on something / when / it is / available / everywhere.

6 People / are more likely / to comply with / the salesmen's persuasion / and / buy a product / when / they think / it is scarce.

7 This "available in limited supply" trick / shows up / everywhere.

8 Whether / we like it or not, / we are / often influenced / by the scarcity effect.

9 Special "limited edition" or "last chance to buy" signs are good examples.

10 But / we / should be wise / enough to know / that the scarce cookie / doesn't actually taste / better.

01 Pi Day

A 다음 영어 표현을 읽고 뜻을 쓰시오.

1 unofficial _____

2 digit _____

3 calculate _____

4 ratio _____

5 circumference _____

6 diameter _____

7 celebration _____

8 concept _____

9 apply _____

10 observe _____

11 accurate _____

12 in addition _____

13 come up with _____

14 gather _____

15 ancient _____

16 assume _____

B 다음 주어진 표현을 배열하여 우리말을 영어로 쓰시오.

1 3월 14일은 미국에 있는 몇몇 사람들의 일상에서 특별한 날이다.

(a special day / in the U.S. / of / in the lives / March 14 / some people / is)

2 고대 그리스의 수학자 아르키메데스는 지름에 대한 원의 둘레의 비율을 계산하여 3.14라는 것을 알아냈다.

(its diameter / of a circle's circumference / the ancient Greek mathematician Archimedes / to / calculated / the ratio)

3 그들이 파이를 먹는 이유 중 하나는 파이와 파이(원주율)라는 단어의 소리가 같기 때문이다.

(they eat pie / one reason / why / is / the words *pie* and *pi* / that / sound the same)

4 어떤 사람들은 파이 데이는 3월 14일보다는 7월 22일에 기념되어야 한다고 말한다. (on July 22 / some people / say / rather than / on March 14 / that / Pi Day / should be observed)

끊어 읽기 구문 학습으로 독해 실력 업그레이드

C 다음과 같이 끊어진 표시에 유의하여 읽고, 문장을 우리말로 해석하시오.

1 It is Pi Day, / an unofficial holiday / celebrating the mathematical constant pi (π).

2 Since / Americans write dates / in order of month and date, / the number 3.14 / stands for / March 14.

3 The first Pi Day celebration / was held in San Francisco / in 1988.

4 Since then, / people around the world / have celebrated the day.

5 They discuss / how the concept of pi / is applied / in daily life.

6 Also, / they have a contest / to see who can say / the most digits / in pi.

7 Since / pi is 3.14159, / the Pi Minute occurs / on March 14 at 1:59 am.

8 According to them, / Archimedes was eventually able to calculate / an even more accurate number / for pi.

9 Instead of 3.14, / he came up with 22/7.

10 On the calendar, / they assume, / 22/7 or July 22 / would be / a better Pi Day.

UNIT
14

02 How Many Digits Are in Pi?

A 다음 영어 표현을 읽고 뜻을 쓰시오.

1	value	_____	9	no matter how	_____
2	digit	_____	10	date back	_____
3	discover	_____	11	figure out	_____
4	mathematician	_____	12	decimal point	_____
5	estimate	_____	13	symbol	_____
6	precise	_____	14	arrival	_____
7	endless	_____	15	repeat	_____
8	series	_____	16	modern	_____

B 다음 주어진 표현을 배열하여 우리말을 영어로 쓰시오.

1 원주율은 원의 둘레와 지름 사이의 비율이다.

(and / Pi / is / between / the ratio / its diameter / the circumference of a circle)

2 오늘날의 원주율 기호(π)는 1706년에 웨일즈의 수학자인 William Jones에 의해 처음 사용되었다.

(was / first used / by Welsh mathematician William Jones / for pi / in 1706 / the modern symbol)

3 원주율에 대한 최초의 기록은 기원전 1900년으로 거슬러 올라간다.

(dates back / of pi / written record / to 1900 BC / the earliest)

4 그것은 모든 사람들이 손으로 원주율의 값을 계산했기 때문이다.

(that / is / by hand / estimated / so because / the value of pie / everyone)

C

끊어 읽기 구문 학습으로 독해 실력 업그레이드

다음과 같이 끊어진 표시에 유의하여 읽고, 문장을 우리말로 해석하시오.

1 Everybody / knows / that the value of pi (π) / is 3.14.

2 In nature, / there are / circles / everywhere.

3 The ratio / is / always the same, / no matter how / big or small a circle is.

4 The Babylonians / figured out / that pi is about 25/8, / while / the Egyptians / came up with / about 256/81.

5 The Greek mathematician Archimedes, / who lived / in the third century BC, / offered 22/7.

6 Pi / was estimated / by one mathematician / after another / over thousands of years.

7 With / the arrival of the computer, / however, / it / became easier / to estimate pi, / and / the value of pi / is / more precise / than ever before.

8 Unlike numbers / such as 3, 9.76, and 10.2387, / pi / has an endless series of numbers / to the right / of the decimal point.

9 Strangely, / the series / never / repeats itself.

10 Mathematicians / have tried / to find a pattern, / but / they / have all failed.

01 Protect the Environment

쉬운 독해를 위한 Vocabulary 업그레이드

A 다음 영어 표현을 읽고 뜻을 쓰시오.

1	extract		9	raw
2	mineral		10	acidic
3	ore		11	wastewater
4	impure		12	impact
5	element		13	get rid of
6	process		14	mine
7	benefit		15	valuable
8	material		16	habitat

B 다음 주어진 표현을 배열하여 우리말을 영어로 쓰시오.

1 채광은 기본적으로 지구에서 광물 광석을 추출하는 것이다.

(from the planet / basically / is / extracting / mining / mineral ores)

2 추출된 광석은 그대로 사용될 수 없다. (are / as / cannot / the extracted ores / be used / they)

3 이것들은 불순물을 제거하기 위해서 주의 깊게 가공되어야 한다.

(the impurities / to / need to / they / be get rid of / carefully processed)

4 채광은 환경에 영향을 미치고, 그래서 세심한 주의를 기울여 행해져야 한다.

(must be undertaken / and / the environment / therefore / impacts / with extreme care / mining)

끊어 읽기 구문 학습으로 독해 실력 업그레이드

C 다음과 같이 끊어진 표시에 유의하여 읽고, 문장을 우리말로 해석하시오.

1 These ores / contain not just the minerals / we are looking for.

2 They also contain / impure elements / that we don't want.

3 This way, / we can get valuable minerals / like gold, silver, aluminum, salt, diamonds, copper, and even uranium.

4 By extracting / and processing the ores, / we get the minerals / that serve as the raw materials / for various products.

5 With the minerals / as raw materials, / we can make an almost countless number of products / which we use / in our daily lives.

6 However, / mining offers benefits / at a price.

7 One big problem / with mining / is acidic wastewater / from mining operations.

8 Acid water can leak / into the nearby soil / and watershed, / dragging poisonous heavy metals / into the ground and surface water.

9 In order to mine, / a large piece of land / must be cleared.

10 Trees are cut down, / and habitats for animals / are destroyed.

UNIT 15

02 The Global Race

쉬운 독해를 위한 Vocabulary 업그레이드

A 다음 영어 표현을 읽고 뜻을 쓰시오.

1	secure	_____	9	global	_____
2	rare	_____	10	export	_____
3	high-tech	_____	11	protect	_____
4	scatter	_____	12	industry	_____
5	bury	_____	13	suffer	_____
6	crust	_____	14	cut back	_____
7	concentrate	_____	15	supply	_____
8	economically	_____	16	usable	_____

B 다음 주어진 표현을 배열하여 우리말을 영어로 쓰시오.

1 국가들은 희토류금속의 안정적인 공급을 위해 바쁘게 움직이고 있다.

(rare earth metals / of / are racing / nations / a secure supply / to have)

2 그것이 희토류금속이 "희귀하다"고 말하는 이유이다.

(rare earth metals / why / "rare" / that is / are called)

3 고도로 집중되어 분포하는 희토류금속 광석은 주로 중국에서 발견된다.

(in China / highly / are / of rare earth metals / usually found / concentrated ores)

4 중국은 자국이 쓸 충분한 희토류금속을 확보하고 자국의 환경을 보호하기 위해 수출량을 줄이고 있다.

(for its own use / China / cutting back / to ensure / it has / export / enough rare earth metals / has been)

C 다음과 같이 끊어진 표시에 유의하여 읽고, 문장을 우리말로 해석하시오.

1 Rare earth metals / are mined / for use / in such high-tech products.

2 For example, / the rare earth metal Holmium / is used to make lasers / while / Promethium is used / to produce nuclear batteries.

3 There are / 17 rare earth metals.

4 They are scattered / across the globe, / and / they are buried / in the planet's crust.

5 But / rare earth metals / are very difficult / to extract.

6 China / is the largest producer / of rare earth metals, / supplying / more than 90 percent / of the global market.

7 Demand / for rare earth metals / worldwide, / however, / grew from / about 85,000 tons in 2003 / to 125,000 tons in 2008.

8 By 2019, / global demand / is expected to / be 1,495,000 tons.

9 Therefore, / it may soon be necessary / to dig / for less concentrated ores / of rare earth metals / in many countries / around the world.

10 If / the demand / for rare earth metals / isn't met, / high-tech industries / may suffer.

A 다음 영어 표현을 읽고 뜻을 쓰시오.

1	philosopher	_____	9	comfort	_____
2	accept	_____	10	spot	_____
3	position	_____	11	vineyard	_____
4	disappointed	_____	12	harvest	_____
5	satisfied	_____	13	palace	_____
6	conclude	_____	14	content	_____
7	cure	_____	15	save	_____
8	cheer up	_____	16	joy	_____

B 다음 주어진 표현을 배열하여 우리말을 영어로 쓰시오.

1 왕은 가능한 모든 방법을 동원해서 그를 기분 좋게 하려고 했다.

(up / tried to / the king / him / with / cheer / every method possible)

2 왕은 그 통치자를 방문해서 무엇이 그를 그렇게 행복하게 하는지를 물었다.

(made / what / and / visited / the king / the ruler / so happy / asked / him)

3 왕은 마음을 달래려 사냥을 나섰다. (the king / to comfort / went out / himself / to hunt)

4 저는 제가 사는 곳을 세상의 어떤 다른 곳과도 바꾸지 않을 것입니다.

(I / for / in the world / wouldn't change / my place / any other place)

끊어 읽기 구문 학습으로 독해 실력 업그레이드

C 다음과 같이 끊어진 표시에 유의하여 읽고, 문장을 우리말로 해석하시오.

1　There / lived / a prince / who was always unhappy.

2　Unable to / look at his son's sad face / any longer, / the king / called for / philosophers, doctors, and professors / to ask for / their advice.

3　After examining / the prince, / the wise men / finally said / to the king.

4　You / must find / a truly happy man, / and / exchange / the prince's shirt / for his.

5　They / found a priest / and brought him / to the king.

6　How / would you like / to accept / a higher position / as my bishop?

7　He / was looking for / a truly happy man / who would not want / more than / what he had.

8　Before long / the king's men brought news / of the ruler / of a neighboring country / where people were satisfied / in peace.

9　Indeed / I / have everything / anybody could possibly want.

10　But / I can't sleep / at night, / worrying about / my death and / losing all I have accomplished.

11 He heard / a man singing a beautiful song / from across a field.

12 Whoever / sings like that / is bound to / be happy!

13 You look / so happy / today!

14 Would you like me / to take you / to the palace?

15 You can enjoy / every kind of comfort / at the palace.

16 No, I'm content with / what I have.

17 At last / I found / a truly happy man! / Now / my son is saved.

18 The king / held the man's hand tight / and / said to the man.

19 Only you / can save / his life.

20 The king / started to open / the young man's jacket.

첫!

내 성적의
비밀에는
이유가 있어

기본 탄탄 나의 첫 중학 내신서

체크체크 전과목 시리즈

국어
공통편·교과서편/학기서

모든 교과서를 분석해 어떤 학교의
학생이라도 완벽 내신 대비

수학
학기서

쉬운 개념부터 필수 개념 문제를
반복 학습하는 베스트셀러

사회·역사
과학
학기서/연간서

전국 기출 문제를 철저히 분석한
학교 시험 대비의 최강자

영어
학기서

새 영어 교과서의 어휘/문법/독해
대화문까지 반영한 실전 대비서

조금 더
공부해
볼까?

배움으로 행복한 내일을 꿈꾸는
천재교육 커뮤니티 안내

· · · ·

 교재 안내부터 구매까지 한 번에!
천재교육 홈페이지

자사가 발행하는 참고서, 교과서에 대한 소개는 물론
도서 구매도 할 수 있습니다. 회원에게 지급되는 별을 모아
다양한 상품 응모에도 도전해 보세요!

 다양한 교육 꿀팁에 깜짝 이벤트는 덤!
천재교육 인스타그램

천재교육의 새롭고 중요한 소식을 가장 먼저 접하고 싶다면?
천재교육 인스타그램 팔로우가 필수!
깜짝 이벤트도 수시로 진행되니 놓치지 마세요!

 수업이 편리해지는
천재교육 ACA 사이트

오직 선생님만을 위한, 천재교육 모든 교재에 대한 정보가 담긴
아카 사이트에서는 다양한 수업자료 및 부가 자료는 물론
시험 출제에 필요한 문제도 다운로드하실 수 있습니다.

https://aca.chunjae.co.kr

 천재교육을 사랑하는 샘들의 모임
천사샘

학원 강사, 공부방 선생님이시라면 누구나 가입할 수 있는 천사샘!
교재 개발 및 평가를 통해 교재 검토진으로 참여할 수 있는 기회는 물론
다양한 교사용 교재 증정 이벤트가 선생님을 기다립니다.

 아이와 함께 성장하는 학부모들의 모임공간
튠맘 학습연구소

튠맘 학습연구소는 초·중등 학부모를 대상으로 다양한 이벤트와 함께
교재 리뷰 및 학습 정보를 제공하는 네이버 카페입니다.
초등학생, 중학생 자녀를 둔 학부모님이라면 튠맘 학습연구소로 오세요!